# EMERGENCY TOUR

# Emergency Tour

## 3 PARA in South Armagh

### PETER MORTON

WILLIAM KIMBER

© Peter Morton 1989

First published in 1989

British Library Cataloguing in Publication data

Morton, Peter
Emergency tour : 3 PARA in South Armagh.
1. Northern Ireland. Freedom movement.
British Army. Retaliation
I. Title
941.60824′092′4

ISBN 0-7183-0687-2

William Kimber & Co Ltd is part of the
Thorsons Publishing Group, Wellingborough,
Northamptonshire, NN8 2RQ, England.

Photoset in North Wales by
Derek Doyle & Associates Mold, Clwyd
and Printed in Great Britain by
Redwood Burn Limited, Trowbridge, Wiltshire

1  3  5  7  9  10  8  6  4  2

# Contents

# Acknowledgements

The first draft of this book was prepared solely for family consumption. The raw material had lain around for ten years and it had become a question of just throwing it all away, or putting it into a more digestible form first. That the project ever really got off the ground is due almost entirely to my personal secretary from 1985-1987, Miss Sheelagh Fitzgerald. During my spasmodic bursts of enthusiasm for the idea, she gave unstintingly of her free time, encouragement and advice to transform a succession of scruffy manuscripts into flawless typescript. I am therefore very much in her debt.

To my surprise, I found in William Kimber a publisher who was prepared to take on the book and with the help of their Amy Myers I then set about transforming it into a work more fit for public interest. Several serving officers and civil servants at the Ministry of Defence, who would prefer to remain anonymous, took the opportunity to read the original and final drafts with care. Their advice was invariably wise, frank, perceptive and consequently helpful, and I am most grateful to them.

Colonel Edward Gardener, Regimental Colonel of The Parachute Regiment, and Richard Hoyle, respectively my second-in-command and adjutant at the time about which I write, were good enough to check the accuracy of the manuscript and they, together with a number of my officers, dug deep into their scrapbooks to produce much of the photographic material. In particular I should like to single out for mention Malcolm Cuthbertson, Richard Gash, Clint Hicks, Tim Hollis and Tony Pugh. Finally on the subject of photographs (and maps) I am indebted to the Controller of Her Majesty's Stationery Office for permission to use the Crown Copyright material.

Despite this assistance from official sources, I must stress that this book has not been given official blessing. Naturally, therefore, the responsibility for the factual accuracy and opinions expressed rests entirely with me.

Peter Morton

# Prologue

On Thursday 15th April 1976 my battalion, the 3rd Battalion of The Parachute Regiment (3 PARA), assumed responsibility for military support to the Royal Ulster Constabulary (RUC) in the southern part of County Armagh, Northern Ireland, an area which is more usually referred to as South Armagh or in the tabloid newspapers as 'bandit country'. The time was 10.07 on a beautiful spring morning and our tour in the country was due to last for four months.

In our various ways we had been looking forward to this moment for some time and the intensive training of the previous two months had been targeted specifically towards it. Spirits were high, mine particularly. I had served in South Armagh before as a company commander in a sister battalion, 2 PARA. That was in 1973 and I had mainly loved it, but some of it was less than amusing. Much had changed in Northern Ireland since then, but in South Armagh the critical factors were unaltered: the countryside was still beautiful, the people were still frightened and generally unhelpful, and our knowledge of the Provisional IRA (PIRA) was still pathetic.

On that April day I had been commanding 3 PARA (consisting of about 650 officers and men) for nearly eight months. It had been a fascinating job thus far which had more than lived up to my high expectations. Our barracks were in Aldershot and we were part of 16 Parachute Brigade, the British Army's sole airborne formation, but we did not seem to spend a great deal of time there. Almost immediately after assuming command I had taken the battalion to the Sudan for a six weeks training period. There we lived rough at the edge of the desert just north of Khartoum, and were the first British troops to visit that amazingly friendly country in any strength since the British presence was withdrawn in 1955. The soldiers quickly became bronzed by the sun and hardened by the living conditions and the very tough training. Morale was sky high and discipline tremendous. Regular Army recruiting at that time was sufficiently good to allow us to reject anyone who failed to measure up to our high standards or who stepped out of line, but few tried it. Everyone in the battalion knew we were off to South Armagh the following spring, and to members of the British Army that represented the most exciting prospect of soldiering available at the time. Certainly nobody who had joined the 'PARAs' could have faced their comrades again if they had missed that Northern Ireland tour without a completely watertight reason.

But it was well before assuming command of 3 PARA that I learnt we would be going to South Armagh in 1976 on what the Army calls an 'emergency' or 'roulement' tour. To those involved this was to mean four months of non-stop (24 hours a day) involvement save for a brief five days R and R (rest and recuperation) period which each individual is permitted once in the four months. This break, which for reasons of manning levels could not be taken by everyone in the middle of the period, would be the only opportunity to see families, be with women, drink or converse with anyone outside the Army except in the line of duty.

In my naïvety I had always assumed that the bright boys in the Ministry of Defence in London had been perceptive in selecting my excellent battalion with myself knowing South Armagh very well as its commanding officer for this tour, and it was only later that I discovered that the officer responsible for making the selections had absolutely no way of knowing anything about the quality and experience of the battalion or its CO. It was perhaps as well that I was so naïve, because I was still then a keen career officer who hoped for a superbly successful 30 months in command of my battalion which would lead inexorably to rapid promotion but I bargained without lady luck (or lack of it), my own deficiencies, and that most unpredictable fellow, the British soldier.

Why I kept a diary I'm not entirely sure. Certainly I regretted not doing so during my previous South Armagh tour

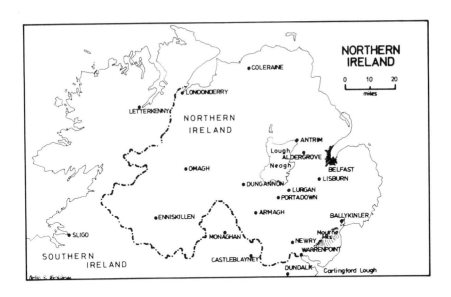

as a company commander in 1973. Then I had responsibility for the large border area which included Forkill, Crossmaglen and Newtownhamilton (see maps on pages 16, 24 and 25) with about 150 men, and although the company had lots of Belfast experience it was almost totally unprepared for the rural area of South Armagh. The previous two months had been spent in Malaysia, our rifles had not even been adjusted (zeroed) to the men, and we had little idea of what to expect. Regrettably, but inevitably, we learnt the hard way. Radio-controlled and electrically detonated landmines occurred with alarming frequency – often several in one day. Four of my soldiers were killed (Company Sergeant Major William Vines, Sergeant John Wallace, Corporal Steven Harrison, Lance Corporal Terence Brown), two more from our armoured car squadron of the 17th/21st Lancers (Corporal Terence Williams and Trooper John Gibbons) and one (Warrant Officer Ian Donald) from the Royal Engineers. I felt their deaths very personally because I knew that with better training and less 'gung-ho' attitude at least some of those men would be alive today. I knew also that several other men had been lucky to escape bomb incidents unscathed. I promised myself therefore that in 1976 things would be different; I now had five times the number of men for an area only twice the size, and I was utterly determined to ensure that no man would be killed through lack of professionalism or awareness, and I was keen also to avenge the deaths of the excellent men lost in 1973.

It was therefore partly to discipline myself that I decided to keep a diary to record what happened, although somewhere at the back of my mind was the thought that it might be interesting to publish a record of the tour at a later date. I knew that to obtain approval for such a publication whilst still serving, and whilst the 'troubles' lasted, would be difficult if not impossible, but as the terrorism had been going on for seven years (since 1969) I reasoned that the end must be in sight. In thinking this way I committed the cardinal sin of underestimating the resilience and longevity of the PIRA who will never achieve their aim of a united Ireland by the cowardly and treacherous methods which they have refined over nearly two decades, but seem prepared to carry on nevertheless. So today, over twelve years later in 1988, terrorism still continues in Northern Ireland. The RUC is very much stronger and in the lead with the Regular Army and the Ulster Defence Regiment (UDR) more and more cast into the supporting role everywhere in the Province except perhaps in the most nationalist border areas. Attacks on security forces, the RUC and especially the regular army, are less frequent but the situation is well removed from what we in mainland Britain could call 'normal', and unfortunately the PIRA can always step up the violence.

Over the more recent years 1979-1984, I have been closely involved with the British Army's reducing manpower commitment to the Province and have viewed with impatience, frustration and often disbelief the ignorant and intemperate rantings of some politicians and journalists on the problems of the border areas and in particular 'cross border co-operation' and 'hot pursuit'. It is high time that some insights into these problems were allowed to surface and I have attempted to achieve this whilst avoiding anything that will put people and techniques at risk, offend the Official Secrets Act, or undermine the government's policy which I wholeheartedly support.

In preparing this account I have faithfully used my diary as an aide memoire, but because much of it was necessarily brief I have naturally had to flesh it out. However, where it is helpful and appropriate I have quoted from it verbatim. It is definitely not an account of all that happened during the tour, to attempt that would be quite impossible, very repetitive and extremely lengthy, but it is not a laundered account either. Instead it is simply 3 PARA's tour, warts and all, through the eyes of its CO.

I hope that this book will help to give some further insight into why most British officers and Civil Servants who have become deeply involved with that troubled Province develop a most curious love hate relationship with it, which is at once fascinating and compulsive yet difficult to rationalise satisfactorily, even to oneself. Certainly I owe it to my friends in the RUC, UDR and the British Army to ensure that this account is objective and fair and I dedicate it to those members of all three whom I knew well, sadly too numerous to list individually, who have given their lives to the just cause of peace in Ulster. Many of them lived and others are still living under the real and ever present threat of assassination and I cannot find words to express my respect and admiration for men and women who are prepared to risk their lives so continuously in order to provide their fellow citizens with the protection to which they are entitled.

Naturally there is adverse comment on individuals and organisations from time to time; to avoid this would be to produce a work which is totally bland. The truth is that every formed body, no matter how good, is bound to have a few rotten apples despite thorough and exhaustive selective processes, and this of course applied just as much to my splendid 3 PARA as to the other groups, several of which had been forced to recruit in great haste. And I am of course writing of the situation in 1976, a year when both the RUC and UDR were at a relatively early stage in their development into the evenhanded and professional organisations which we know them to be today. No matter how amateur some of their efforts may have seemed to me then, their personal commitment, bravery, humour, good intentions and seemingly limitless patience were never in question.

Most particularly I dedicate this account to my wife Paddy, who has loyally followed the flag and supported me and the

British Army for 28 years. There have been few perks in her life as she has been frequently abandoned at home with our three daughters as I was whisked around the world. Nevertheless, she provided an immaculately run and vitally secure haven to which I could always return sure in the knowledge that nothing would be amiss. Few men are so fortunate. She was especially important during the Northern Ireland tour about which I write when she, together with my families officer, Mick Edney, kept motherly and fatherly eyes on the 300 or so families who remained behind in the Aldershot area. One subject I never had to give more than a moment's thought to was our families; they were in very safe hands indeed.

# CHAPTER ONE

# The Task

3 PARA is an infantry battalion which is trained to go to war by parachute. But because parachuting, and especially military parachuting, requires special physical and mental qualities, The Parachute Regiment is permitted to be more exactingly selective than other infantry regiments in the British Army. Whilst an infantry battalion is a fighting machine consisting of about 650 regular soldiers each of whom has a mind of his own and a physical break point, so Parachute battalions are of similar size but are composed of individuals whose mental and physical qualities are on average higher up the scale, whose general attitude is more aggressive, and whose approach to life and death is somewhat more fatalistic.

However, soldiering in Northern Ireland is certainly not about aggression, nor fatalism, and indeed many would argue that it is not really soldiering at all. Belfast is almost as far removed from real soldiering as it is possible to get, but in South Armagh many of the tasks demand highly developed infantry skills and country craft. But wherever a battalion goes in Northern Ireland it needs certain organisational changes and a lot of re-training to make it fit for its unfamiliar role. The fighting machine must be broken up into individuals and small teams who can think and operate sensitively, intelligently and always within the law no matter how provocative or frightening the situation in which they find themselves.

In late 1975 3 PARA was organised with a Battalion Headquarters (HQ), three Rifle Companies (A, B, C), Patrol Company, Support Company and HQ Company. The total strength of 40 officers and 610 soldiers was divided amongst the six companies, each of which was commanded by a Major

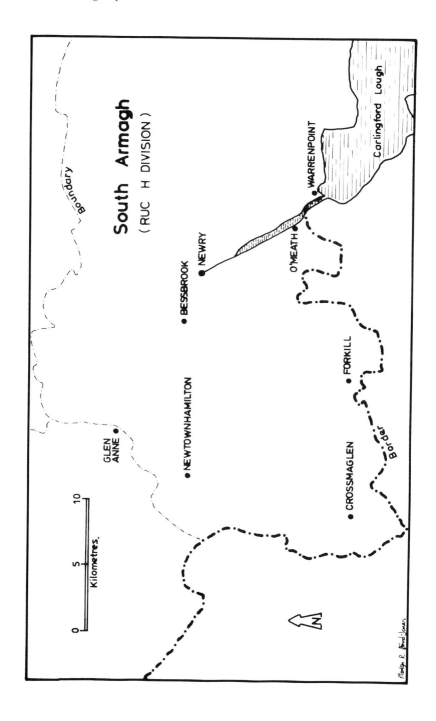

known as the company commander or OC (officer command-ing). These companies were essentially different in character. Patrol Company, smaller than the others, contained carefully selected volunteers who were patient, self-reliant and especially suited to covert surveillance work. Support Company, on the other hand, consisted of experienced soldiers cast in a tougher and more gregarious mould. The youngest and least experienced men were in the Rifle Companies where their fitness and agility were important. Finally the more staid members of the battalion tended to have eased themselves into the more sedentary jobs connected with the command function (Battalion HQ) or administration (HQ Company). This then was the highly trained 3 PARA which flew back from the Sudan just in time for Christmas leave in 1975. I was confident that it was the best battalion in the Army but by early April 1976 it had to be transformed in both structure and attitude.

Everyone with any knowledge of the British Army will understand that its infantry battalions are very much tight knit units in which the officers and men know each other and their families, well. But for all their camaraderie they are still a bunch of individuals each of whom will react differently to his neighbour in a given situation. Unlike ships or aircraft where, willy-nilly, everyone on board must change course when the captain decides to, the CO of an infantry battalion has far less control. Indeed the esteem of his unit is often totally dependent on the actions of the most inexperienced or stupid of his soldiers. So fine tuning such a body is very much a management skill and the first essential is to get the officers and SNCOs into the appointments which best suit their particular talents. Success in this complex matrix can produce a beautiful smooth-running machine, failure will result in something which is less appealing.

In the British Army we are obviously not in the hire and fire business so an individual officer or SNCO continues to serve for the length of his contract even though he may have been promoted above his natural ceiling. Each of these individuals had his strong points and his weak points which were furthermore complicated by the rank he held and by the fact that a hierarchical organisation like an Army is very sensitive that jobs and rank are related. So as a CO I could only juggle with what I had available, but juggle one must for in this case I had to create from within the battalion three groups which were not needed for our normal life of training for general war.

The first was a team of about twenty (officers and men) capable of handling and disseminating intelligence, the second was a command and standby system capable of instant response 24 hours a day for four months, and the third was a group to run what was then (before the North Sea oil boom) the busiest heliport in Europe at the battalion's HQ in Bessbrook, near Newry. All this without weakening the 'fighting' companies in the process which meant trimming administration to the bone and borrowing from any other unit in our brigade who had someone they wished to volunteer for the experience. I was also helped in this business by an agreement to restrict postings into and out of the battalion for the duration of the four months of the tour and the three months training which preceded it; these postings normally run at a rate of well over 100 in a year, although as will be seen a number of key members of staff were to change over in the course of the tour. In addition I had to leave a handful of people behind in Aldershot to caretake our barracks and look after our essential interests there.

In early January 1976 selected officers and men were despatched from Aldershot to attend specialist courses on subjects which would be vital to our role in Northern Ireland – for example, intelligence processing, terrorist recognition and search techniques – whilst on the 19th I, together with my Intelligence Officer (IO), took the shuttle from Heathrow to Northern Ireland for my first look since 1973 at the problems which we would be facing in April. We were met at Aldergrove, then still a very simple, soulless, heavily guarded and consequently deserted airport, and taken to HQ 3 Infantry Brigade at Lurgan where I was greeted by an old friend, Major H. Jones (later to gain a posthumous Victoria Cross for his action in command of 2 PARA in the Falklands in 1982). Also there for briefing was the commanding officer of 22 SAS as my visit coincided with the first official public announcement by the Labour Government that the SAS were to be deployed to Northern Ireland and specifically to South Armagh as a response to the vicious sectarian attacks of that period. The

*Bessbrook Mill: the area covered by the lower photograph is marked on the upper photograph* (Upper photograph, Crown copyright).

brigade commander, Brigadier David Anderson, spared me a little of his precious time before I was whisked off to Bessbrook, home of the battalion responsible for South Armagh, and from whom 3 PARA would be taking over. This was 1st Battalion The Royal Scots (1 RS) whose CO, Lieutenant Colonel Philip Davies, I'd never met before but had seen on a BBC TV programme a few weeks previously where he had impressed me. In real life he was tall, personable and self-assured, and was luckily blessed with a good team at Bessbrook where the whole place seemed reasonably clean, efficient and cheerful.

That was no mean achievement because the Bessbrook base is a slice of an old linen mill which has been largely empty for several decades but since 1969 parts have been converted, reconverted and converted again for the stream of Army units who have been living there. Building work consisting principally of the erection of hardboard partitions hardly ever seemed to stop, and the whole place was consequently a worrying fire risk and something of a rabbit warren. Drains which were once barely adequate for the factory workforce during the working day were grossly overtaxed as they struggled to cope with the demands of up to 500 men living permanently on the site.

My stay with 1 RS was to be brief but most useful. I visited each of the battalion's principal outstations by Sioux helicopter. Three of these were established in RUC stations (Forkill, Crossmaglen, and Newtownhamilton) and two in UDR centres (Newry and Glenanne). The way these bases had evolved over the preceding years depended on the circumstances surrounding each and was certainly not the result of some grand design. For example the three RUC stations (always called barracks by the locals) were identical whitewashed two storey buildings with a few small offices on the ground floor and a number of bedrooms above, how many I could not say because by 1976 they had been altered almost unrecognisably from the original design. Early in the campaign Forkill and Crossmaglen RUC stations had been taken over almost totally by the Army and the very few RUC constables who remained were virtual prisoners who could only leave by courtesy of the garrison. On the other hand at Newtownhamilton, a much more Protestant area to the north end of South Armagh proper, a large degree of normal

**Above** *Helicopters landing and taking off.*

**Below** *The Mill from the HLS.*

**Above** *Radio antennae on the roof.*

**Below** *Fences and anti-rocket screens.*

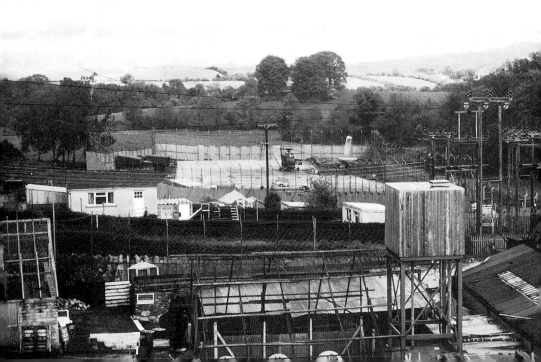

routine police work was still possible.

In 1973 when I had first been responsible for the area I had had a platoon (30 men) in each Forkill and Newtownhamilton, and a further 60 at Crossmaglen. Now 1 RS had a company of about 120 men in each. Naturally this number could not be squeezed into buildings originally designed to house a handful of constables without alteration and discomfort, so a variety of portable buildings had been introduced and these ranged from garden sheds, through Portakabins to custom-built extensions. The result was untidy and extremely cramped.

1 RS deployment was in sum Forkill (one company), Crossmaglen (one company), Newtownhamilton (one company less one platoon), Glenanne (one company of the Spearhead battalion), Bessbrook (one Spearhead company) and Newry (one company plus an additional platoon making a total of four). My general impression from the visit was that 1 RS was generously well off for soldiers because of the additional two Spearhead companies they had attached to them (another response to the sectarian violence) but I considered that the type of terrorist activity had not changed much since my last visit in 1973 although the quantity of it had reduced, and certainly the level of intelligence about the terrorists was the same (ie virtually non-existent).

As a result of this visit I was in a position to decide tentatively how I would deploy 3 PARA when my turn came in April. I could not expect the Spearhead companies to remain in Northern Ireland until then, so I ignored the possibility that they might and made my plan as follows:

A Company (Colin Thomson with 3 platoons)
                                  – Crossmaglen
B Company (Ian Chapman with 2 platoons)
                                  – Newtownhamilton
C Company (Malcolm Cuthbertson with 2 platoons)
                                  – Forkill
Patrol Company (Roger Miller)        – Bessbrook
Support Company (Joe Baker with 3 platoons)
                                  – Newry
SAS Squadron              – Bessbrook
Two platoons (one from each B and C Companies)
                                  – Bessbrook

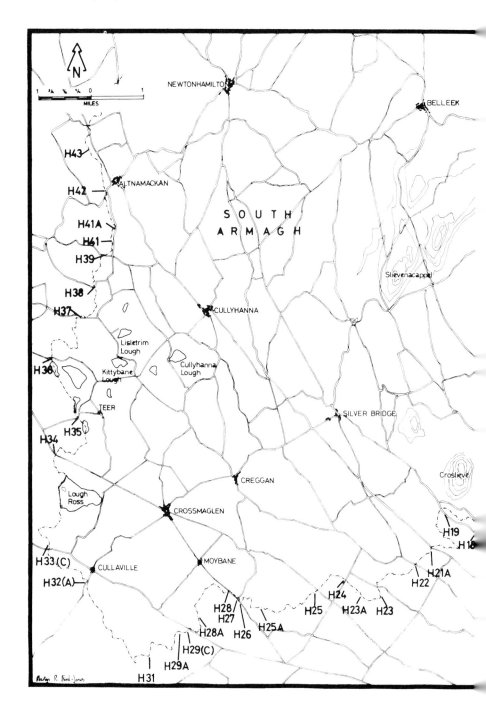

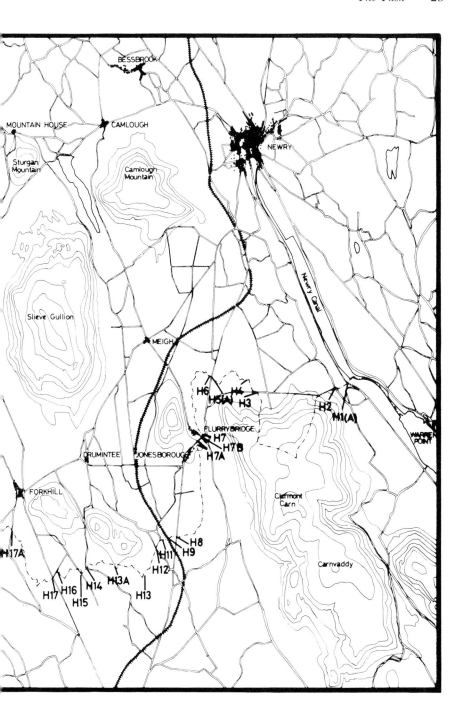

*Forkill Base* (Upper photograph, Crown copyright).

Three weeks later, on 8th February, I returned to Northern Ireland for the main reconnaissance. On this occasion I was accompanied by my principal staff and administrative officers and all the company commanders – a total of thirteen. The party met at Heathrow. Major Colin Thomson, who was to command A Company, was joining 3 PARA for the first time direct from the MOD where he had been driving a desk and Majors Ian Chapman and Roger Miller (B and Patrol Companies respectively) re-joined on completion of a long course at the School of Infantry at Warminster in Wiltshire. As a result of these late arrivals I had had no opportunity to get the party together to talk to them so we were a pretty unco-ordinated bunch and our group resembled a reunion more than a serious reconnaissance party.

On arrival at Aldergrove the routine was much as before but on this occasion as there were more of us, we travelled to HQ 3 Infantry Brigade in Lurgan in a most obvious Army Bedford bus. I remember clearly thinking how vulnerable we were, we had not a weapon between us and it would have been a splendid propaganda coup for one of the terrorist organisations to wipe out the complete hierarchy of a battalion. Safely at our destination however H. Jones and a small team briefed us before we again piled into the coach for an even more perilous trip to Bessbrook which we reached in time for lunch. There my immediate priority was to talk to the whole party myself before each individual set off to examine and absorb the task for which he would become responsible in April.

On the second day, Tuesday, I spent my time moving around the company bases by helicopter where I found my own company commanders looking suitably intrigued and not a little bewildered by the situation in which they found themselves. For myself I was able to spend quite a time with Lieutenant Colonel Philip Davies, the outgoing CO, which I found extremely valuable. It confirmed many of my pre-conceived notions and I was again impressed by his expressed determination to get to grips with the PIRA.

On Wednesday I had an amusing day. It had snowed quite hard overnight and the strong wind had a devastating ability to penetrate clothing. I went first by Sioux to visit HMS *Alert* in Carlingford Lough, the beautiful sea lough that forms the south-eastern boundary between Northern and Southern Ireland. *Alert* is a tiny converted motor fishing vessel run by the Royal Navy which is stationed in the Lough to deter smuggling across its tidal waters. It is too small to land a helicopter on, so I was dropped on the beach and picked up by two 'rigid raiders'. These are the dories, powered by large outboard engines which the Royal Marines detachment, part of *Alert*'s complement, used to patrol and to intercept suspicious vessels. Fortunately they gave me a 'dry suit', for we set off at full throttle and a cloud of icy spray up the choppy Lough. Space on board *Alert* was at a premium but we squeezed into a tiny cabin where I perched on the bunk. A steaming mug of coffee was thrust into my grateful hand and I was quickly put into the picture by the two RN and RM officers and an hour later, clad once more in my 'dry suit', I left to visit the UDR.

The UDR at that time consisted of eleven battalions commanded by British Army regular lieutenant-colonels supported by a few key people also from the regular army. The remainder of each battalion consisted exclusively of Northern Irishmen and women, the majority of whom were part-time soldiers. Although the British Government's original intention was to recruit a UDR which would faithfully reflect the two religious groupings in Ulster, the regiment did in fact by 1976 consist almost wholly of Protestants, the Catholics having been discouraged by terrorist action and intimidation from joining. This was easily done especially in those UDR battalions which recruited in one of the four border counties of Londonderry, Tyrone, Fermanagh and Armagh. Anyone (man or woman) from those counties joining the UDR, or for that matter the RUC, immediately put at risk their own lives and those of their near relatives 24 hours a day, 365 days a year, and the wonder is not that so few joined but that so many are still prepared to take up the challenge. Nevertheless and despite the government's good and honest intentions, the UDR has inevitably become a force which is loathed by the extreme Catholics and adored by the extreme Protestants.

These were early days for the UDR and they were largely very enthusiastic but also very amateur. Today they are much more highly trained and more even handed and my comments about them in later chapters would not be justified today. However one

*Crossmaglen Base.* (Upper photograph, Crown copyright).

thing has not altered and that is the largely unsung bravery of men and women who willingly and voluntarily risk their lives so constantly for a cause which they believe in – the democratic rights of their fellow citizens in the torn country of Northern Ireland.

Each UDR battalion was responsible for providing military support in an area of the Province, and there were two UDR battalion areas which abutted onto the South Armagh regular battalion's tactical area of responsibility (TAOR) and it was these two that I had to visit. The first was 3 UDR at Ballykinler, just north of Newcastle, County Down and the shortest route from Carlingford Lough was along the eastern side of the Mountains of Mourne into the teeth of the north-easterly gale. Our ground speed seemed to get slower and slower, and as we reached the point where the Mournes drop into the sea we started to slip backwards. There was no alternative but to turn tail and go around the western side of the mountains thus avoiding the worst of the gale. My arrival therefore was rather late but still time enough to get a useful feel for 3 UDR. The CO, Lieutenant Colonel Ian McCausland, a large, imposing and gregarious officer gave me a completely honest appraisal of his battalion which at that stage in its evolution he regarded more as a militia than a professional military force. He advised that when and if I made use of his company which was located within the South Armagh battalion's TAOR I should be cautious and restrict that use to their local knowledge which in terms of terrorist familiarity was poor as they were recruited from a largely Unionist area, and to their skill in conducting vehicle check points (VCPs).

Back into the Sioux with the gale on our tail we made short work of the distance to Armagh city. There the CO of 2 UDR, Lieutenant Colonel Richard Elliot, made it quite clear to me that his battalion was a very much more advanced organisation than 3 UDR which may have owed much to their recruiting area which was rather more mixed in religious terms. 2 UDR was clearly keen on becoming involved in patrol tasks, specifically within South Armagh, and he also stressed their intelligence gathering potential which was evidently quite good as many of his soldiers lived and worked amongst convinced Nationalists.

Finally, to conclude this round of visits I went to Newry RUC station, a substantial brick building in the backstreets of Newry, transformed into something of a bastion by corrugated iron, barbed wire and concrete, which is the HQ for the Royal Ulster Constabulary's H Division. The Chief Superintendent and the Head of Special Branch (HSB) were old friends and both seemed pleased to see me and I was certainly pleased to see them. I had a long wide ranging chat with the Chief Superintendent who inter alia confirmed my opinion that closing border crossing roads was totally counter productive and that improvised explosive devices (IEDs) – landmines etc – on or near the border could remain in position and need not be defused in a hurry. These were important matters as they would affect our training and a digression here on these two subjects is therefore appropriate.

First, 'sealing the border'. How often over the last almost two decades have we heard this expression, more usually from the more extreme of Ulster's Loyalist politicians, but often also from seemingly responsible figures, inside and outside Ulster, of all political persuasions. But what do they mean? Northern Ireland's border with the South is 303 miles long and except in a few places follows no geographic logic. It splits communities and farms straddle it. Worldwide the only effective borders are those where the natural geography is very inhospitable (eg between Chile and Argentina) or where access is denied by physical construction (such as the border between East and West Germany). Ireland, North and South, is an area of friendly undulating pasture divided into small fields by overgrown and in many cases pretty impenetrable blackthorn hedges. Roads and tracks abound and can in any event be easily constructed. Physical barriers such as rivers running conveniently in the right direction, unfathomable bogs, or thick forest and high mountains are almost completely absent.

The border is crossed by at least 291 roads and tracks most of which are passable to ordinary motor cars, some of these are deemed 'approved crossings' and in South Armagh they were indicated on maps by the simple designation H1 to H43 (the H stood for the RUC's H Division). In the early 1970s, attempts were made to reduce this number with limited success, but in those places where communities on one side normally focussed on the other (for example South Armagh where Dundalk and Castleblaney not Newry are the traditional foci), blocking a road served only to alienate opinion on both sides and of course unless a blocked crossing can be permanently guarded it is child's play with an excavator to reopen it.

Naturally the border could be guarded, it would take a lot of men and material but it could be done, the Soviets have shown that. However, it is democracy, and the right of every group of people in a community to voice an opinion without discrimination, that we are pledged to defend in Northern Ireland, so a physical barrier would be entirely at odds with that principle, and of course if you have a physical barrier the only way to cut down the number of men required to protect it is to do as the Soviets have done in East Germany. That border is 870 miles long or nearly three times the length of the border in Ireland. We do not know how many border guards we would need to provide a barrier to Soviet standards but to translate East Germany into Ulster would demand 303 miles of mesh fencing, 6-metre wide ploughed and harrowed strip, vehicle track, and Hinterland security fence. To these must be added about 360,000 explosive charges, 165 miles of vehicle hazards (ditches and dragon's teeth), 100 pill boxes, 100 concrete observation towers, command posts, earth bunkers, dogs and dog runs, arc lights etc.

Clearly that is unacceptable so the only pragmatic solution to the border is to reduce its impact, to make conditions on both sides so similar that traffic across it is not caused by political and economic differences. Sadly today, despite the South joining the EEC, economic differences are now sharper than they have ever been and the ecumenical movement, on which so much depends, is still regrettably in its infancy.

Now to the second digressionary point, IEDs in the border area. On my previous tour in 1973 the policy was that 'normality' was to be the watchword. We used helicopters, but also used the roads routinely in both civilian and military vehicles. The PIRA had decided to drive us off the roads and away from the border area by killing soldiers and RUC policemen especially by the clever use of landmines triggered remotely, and often from within the Republic. This situation over a period of a few years forced almost all security force

*Views of typical South Armagh countryside.*

traffic off the roads, prevented routine police activities and removed the Customs and Excise. South Armagh became an area where the norm was anarchy, not the rule of law. As each landmine was discovered, there was in 1973 pressure from within the Army and the public to defuse them quickly, but by 1976 when security forces no longer needed roads for their own routine movement this pressure had been removed. Unquestionably this was a blessing because it eliminated the need constantly to patrol the roads and to mount IED clearance operations at short notice when landmines were found or suspected.

Although never a 'no go' area, South Armagh was effectively under the bully-boy control of the PIRA, and it probably still is. In this situation smuggling, traditionally a normal pursuit of the local population, has prospered. I remember well in 1973, sitting inconspicuously in a helicopter, watching the smuggling activities of one farmer, whose operations I reported to the Customs and Excise, but no action was taken.

On my way back to England I stopped at RAF Aldergrove for a quick chat with Wing Comander Keith Harding who commanded the support helicopter (Puma and Wessex) squadron on which the South Armagh battalion so totally relies for administration and operational deployment. He was extremely helpful and constructive which augured well. My experience in the Parachute Regiment had taught me many years before that the Army and RAF often misunderstood one another. Indeed it was always half jokingly said in the regiment that our additional pay was not danger money for parachute duties but for being 'buggered about' by the RAF. In any event we often seemed to have different priorities and senses of value which I suppose stemmed from the fact that the RAF is equipment orientated and their manpower is solely there to crew and maintain aircraft, whereas the Army and the infantry in particular are people orientated, equipping men rather than the other way round. To us in the Army the RAF officers all too often seemed to be very hide-bound and reluctant to 'have a go'. Although true in some instances this was an appallingly unfair generalisation and could rarely be levelled at the vast majority of front-line pilots. Anyway it was vital that for our forthcoming tour 3 PARA and the RAF support helicopter squadron were absolutely in harmony, a situation which I felt we could achieve only if we worked hard to foster it.

In this context I had already made what would prove to be an inspired decision. It had been recommended to me that the vital job of ensuring the smooth running of Bessbrook heliport should be entrusted to a senior officer, but I had decided to give the job instead to an old and staunch ally in the battalion, Warrant Officer Kane. I was confident that he was just the man to deal effectively and sympathetically with the wide range of pilot ranks (from wing commander to sergeant), with the airborne standby force (normally commanded by a corporal), and all the other people involved in sending stores or men by air to the distant parts of the battalion. In the event his unruffled charm led to a marvellously trusting relationship between aircrew and passengers which was to be a major contribution to the success of our tour.

# CHAPTER TWO

# Training

An obligatory part of each unit's preparation for Northern Ireland is a training package guided by the British Army's Northern Ireland Training and Advisory Team (NITAT). In December I had decided that serious training for our tour would not start before the team's formal visit to the battalion in Aldershot which I programmed for the week 16th-20th February 1976. This allowed just eight weeks of concentrated training – more than enough if we were to peak at the right time and not go off the boil as some units were inclined to.

The NITAT was led by Major Sandy Lindsay of The Black Watch and he and I had agreed that 3 PARA should be given all the standard presentations and training but slanted towards operations in a rural area. Everyone in the battalion attended this training, much of which was in lecture form. Having no place in my own barracks to seat over 600 men we used instead Maida Gymnasium, a large brick-built Victorian building, draughty enough to ensure full attention, but just warm enough to prevent unnecessary discomfort.

I was impressed by the instructional package. The teaching standards were very high and seemed to strike the right balance. By the end of the week everyone in the battalion had been brought up to date on the current situation in Ulster, on the Republican and Loyalist terrorist organisations and on their weapons, equipment and tactics. They had grasped the rudiments of the legal procedure and arrest formalities, and they had practised, under instruction, a number of security force techniques such as searching buildings and individuals, VCPs, terrorist recognition and the rules of minimum force as contained in the Yellow Card (the aide memoire carried by all soldiers in Northern Ireland to remind them of points of law and especially when they could and could not use lethal force). A most valuable part of the whole week was a talk by the Newry RUC Superintendent who impressed my soldiers very much indeed and he came across to them as the caring, unbiased, thoughtful and even-handed policeman that I knew him to be.

On 24th February, the Brigadier commanding 16 Parachute Brigade, Geoffrey Howlett, visited 3 PARA in our Aldershot barracks for the battalion's annual inspection. It was very informal and consisted of little more than a walk around every nook and cranny in the battalion with him affably asking penetrating questions of my officers and men, but it was very good for us to have got this ritual out of the way, and so satisfactorily. The deck was then clear to concentrate exclusively on our work-up training for South Armagh.

Two days later, on the 26th, I spoke to all the officers and NCOs. I talked about the PIRA tactics for killing and maiming soldiers in South Armagh and I reminded them that on average only one PIRA terrorist had died for every 50 British soldiers who had lost their lives there. I stressed that although we had to attempt to achieve a much better record we must treat the local population politely, sensitively and sympathetically, no matter what the provocation. I also gave them six points to concentrate on during the ensuing weeks of training. These were: map reading (with a border so irregular and unmarked, and with so much hanging on accuracy, map reading had to be perfect); shooting (opportunities to engage terrorists would be very infrequent and brief, and there would be no second chances); patrolling skills; covert observation post (COP) skills; ambush skills; and finally, alertness. These of course were purely military skills which would overlay all the special to Northern Ireland techniques which we would be learning and refining.

Normally the sequence of preparatory training for battalions bound for South Armagh was to spend two weeks on specialist ranges in Kent followed by a week in Norfolk on a rural exercise which was designed to serve as a final rehearsal of everything that we could expect in Ulster. In our case this sequence had to be reversed due to the unavailability of the rural training area (because of heavy demand by other units) at the right time, so it meant that we went there not at the end of our training but near the beginning of it. This was unfortunate but not disastrous and we proceeded there for the period 27th February-5th March.

The Norfolk training area is a delightful oasis of pasture, forest, lake and deciduous woodland teeming in wildlife, including that rare animal the red squirrel, but it is nothing like South Armagh. By using the camps set around the periphery as 'bases' and a great deal of imagination some semblance of a rural exercise could be produced and I noted in my diary that although our efforts there were pretty chaotic to begin with, we improved as we went along. The umpires we took with us were superb, and their use of close circuit television to replay an event was a very convincing training aid and method of debriefing. I finished the week with 25 serious points that needed remedying before April and the umpires gave me another twelve. Over the following two weeks I left it to company commanders to address all of these points in the local Aldershot training areas.

A number of individual and group specialists upon whom we would need to place great reliance during our tour were not with us at this stage of our training. Most were represented by others with similar skills as those who would actually be attached to the battalion or work intimately with us were already in Ulster. Such people were the Ammunition Technical Officer whose role was the disposal of any terrorist explosive device. He was a member of the Royal Army Ordnance Corps, normally a senior NCO but sometimes an officer, and always supported by a small number of operators. They were a very brave band, particularly those who had to work in South Armagh where the terrorists were the most innovative.

The Royal Engineers provided a small team under a SNCO who were especially skilled in search techniques and their role was to find a clear and safe route to a device and then hand over to ATO who would actually destroy or defuse it. Dogs and dog handlers were also useful in this regard and at Bessbrook we would have several 'sniffer' dogs (usually labradors) who were trained (with a handler, a volunteer soldier) to sniff out explosives, and one bloodhound, a magnificent specimen whose handler hardly matched him for enthusiasm or stamina.

In addition a group of Women's Royal Army Corps girls were available to us 'on call' for use on those occasions when we might need to search females. Lastly, in Northern Ireland, each of us in management would have to lean heavily on the advice and guidance of our RUC opposite numbers, and although a token number were brought over for the exercise they were too inexperienced to reproduce the arguments and help which would be available in Ulster – nevertheless, they were much better than nothing.

One of the seemingly trivial, but nonetheless important matters which I had to consider at this early stage was how we should present ourselves to the public in Northern Ireland. In other words how we should kit out the few vehicles we would use and what we should wear. It may seem extraordinary that we had any choice in this but surprisingly it was left to each battalion to decide; in the British infantry 'uniform' is very much a question of individual choice.

The vehicle question was very easy. Traditionally during the Regiment's many tours in Ulster we had refused to use the issue armour plating for the landrovers preferring instead to strip off the canopies so that the vehicles could become mobile observation platforms from which the passengers could easily both handle their weapons and dismount. I saw no reason to break with this well established tradition.

I was also dead against the flak jackets (body armour). They were of American design and although satisfactory for static tasks they were very limiting in a mobile situation. They were bulky, heavy, and in the summer excessively hot, and in my experience they had an adverse effect on the alertness and agility of the wearer. My soldiers shared my dislike of them so my decision not to wear them except in static sentry positions was greatly welcomed. There was another reason for taking this line which was essentially pragmatic. The jackets provided some protection against stones, shrapnel and low velocity bullets but virtually none against the two principal weapons we would encounter in South Armagh, namely the large bomb and the high velocity bullet.

Finally I considered it important to continue to wear our famous maroon berets and of course if we did, it would also be wholly inappropriate to use camouflage cream on our faces as was the custom on rural patrols. However, I could not order that berets be worn if by doing so I would place my soldiers at increased risk by making them more visible to the terrorists. Obviously we could not wear our silver cap badges so a black version was substituted, and I then arranged a simple trial to see if the maroon colour and white face was a particular disadvantage amongst the fields and hedgerows. To my great delight the trial proved conclusively that at any distance in excess of about 200 metres, it was movement not colour which first attracted attention, a conclusion which would come as no surprise to a bird watcher or game keeper. Unquestionably the smartly dressed soldier in his beret and with his face clearly visible was at a considerable advantage when talking to the locals if compared with other members of the Army who often looked unnecessarily warlike.

On 21st March we went to Kent for the two weeks' training package which should have preceded our rural exercise; it was to prove invaluable. The training area had been developed over the previous six years, since the start of the British Army's commitment to Northern Ireland, into a highly sophisticated range complex which is today unequalled anywhere in the world. The emphasis is on shooting (especially in an urban environment), observation, and riot control – a skills package more valuable to a battalion posted to Belfast or Londonderry than to South Armagh. Nevertheless, it provided unique opportunity to change the mental attitude of soldiers and attune them to the sensitivities of arrest procedure, restraint, patrolling within a civilian community, vehicle check point procedures and instantaneous and correct reaction to suspicious activity or an actual attack. Most of the detail I left to my excellent second-in-command, Major Edward Gardener, and spent much of my time fending off visitors (although on 29th March we were delighted to host our Regimental Colonel Commandant, General Sir Roland Gibbs and the Deputy Commander of United Kingdom Land Forces, Lieutenant-General Sir Hugh Beach), and wandering around the range complex watching, encouraging and correcting the companies in their training.

Several of the companies showed signs of considerable inexperience. One of the most enjoyable exercises was one in which one company patrols and reacts to events in an urban area whilst another, dressed in plain clothes plays the part of the locals and terrorists. The plain clothes role was the most popular not least because WRAC volunteers were provided to play the part of girlfriends and wives. Inevitably some of the 'acting' was most realistic. Support Company showed themselves to be somewhat provocative and heavy-handed and I had to make it clear to them that their responses would not be acceptable in Newry.

During the fortnight I was also training and educating myself. I spent two days at the home of the SAS being briefed on all their capabilities which was totally fascinating and I also spent one day at Beaconsfield undergoing a very short course in TV interview technique, training against the unlikely event that I would have to face a camera crew in Ulster. Finally I was sorting out the battalion's personalities. One young officer was replaced and there were a few changes amongst the senior NCOs.

I had earlier despatched the first advance party together with my intelligence sections under the IO to Ulster where they were already settling in. There was a small team at each company location and a larger one at Bessbrook. They had several weeks to immerse themselves into the scene so that they knew all the personalities and took over every grain of knowledge that was in the heads of their predecessors in 1 RS.

One or two of the company teams were headed by officers I had 'borrowed' from elsewhere in the Parachute Brigade and one such was a very young officer of the Royal Electrical and Mechanical Engineers. He was very inexperienced but keen to learn and anxious to make his mark. It was his first time in Northern Ireland. I received a frantic telephone call on 29th March from Philip Davies in Bessbrook to say that this young man had made a complete nonsense at Forkill and must be removed immediately. Apparently he and his small team had been invited by the RUC Sergeant at Forkill to visit the local public house with him and because they were anxious to get on well with the RUC and to meet some of the locals, they had agreed. It was of course an extremely silly thing to do where such an act was to invite assassination and it was most unusual for an RUC officer to behave in such a daring way in South

Armagh. However, it was an act of inexperience rather than stupidity but Philip was quite insistent and put the officer on the first 'plane back to England. This was unnecessary, he was in Forkill to learn the ropes from the outgoing unit and it was they who in my view were almost as much at fault in this instance.

Undaunted, he was to return with the main body a fortnight later to start what turned out to be a thoroughly useful tour but the incident alerted me to the thought that perhaps 1 RS were not as assured as first impressions had led me to believe. Three days later three soldiers from 1 RS were killed in an explosion. These were their first deaths and as a battalion they sadly joined all who had preceded them in South Armagh as having suffered fatal casualties.

On Tuesday 6th April I heard the bad news that the officer whom I had selected as my operations officer, Major Pat Conn, a very experienced person with a deep insight into intelligence work also, had hurt his back again (a recurring parachuting injury) and was in hospital. So there we were, four days before leaving for Ulster, with no operations officer. It was a serious blow but at that stage I did not know how bad Pat's problem would be. Mentally crossing my fingers I weighed up the possibilities which seemed to be either to take Roger Miller from command of Patrol Company or to use the second-in-command of the Forkill Company, Captain Andrew Dudzinski, and replace him there with someone else. I visited Pat in hospital where I found him in traction, but there was no positive news.

On Thursday 8th April I addressed the whole battalion at 08.30, and made six specific points to them:

1. South Armagh is a dangerous place. No unit had ever served there without losing some men and it was therefore quite vital that everyone had checked that the details of their next of kin were correct. (This opening gambit had the merit of concentrating everyone's attention.)

2. That if we were to score any success ourselves we must go out and seek it. I made the soccer analogy that if we just defended we would eventually let in a goal and certainly would not score any ourselves.

*WRAC personnel and dog handlers returning home after a dawn search.*

3. That we all had to be ready for a contact with terrorists at every instant, waking and sleeping, during the next four months. There would be no second chances and no time to cogitate.

4. That we must treat the local population well no matter how rude, unco-operative or provocative they might be. I reminded them that even the worst Irishmen and women would find it difficult to behave badly if we were always unfailingly polite.

5. That we sought success which would only come with a blend of skill and luck.

6. That any success, so rare was it in South Armagh, would have far-reaching effects.

Finally, I wished them well and went off to take my leave of my brigade commander, Geoffrey Howlett, who had been my CO during my previous South Armagh tour. Later that morning I learnt that Pat Conn would not be in Ulster at all and I thus telephoned Andrew Dudzinski in Forkill, promoted him instantly to acting Major, and told him of his new appointment.

Then I rang Philip Davies to warn him of the change – he sounded very fraught.

Two days later, on Saturday 10th April, I left Aldershot with my full advance party of about 100 officers and men. Most went by coach and rail to Liverpool whilst I travelled with Corporal Mitchum, my excellent driver, and trusted companion in a car which had been painted a most unusual shade of blue for the occasion, supposedly to make it unrecognisable as an Army staff car. In explanation I was told that the workshop had no authority to purchase quality cellulose but it might as well have been painted in Army green and black camouflage, it was still so obviously a military car. We sailed at dusk in the landing ship *Sir Lancelot* and enjoyed a very calm, cheerful and uneventful passage to Belfast where we docked early the following morning on a typically wet and dismal Ulster Sunday.

# CHAPTER THREE

# Pause for Thought

## *11th-14th April 1976*

By 11.00 we were all at Bessbrook. The company advance
parties were whisked off to their bases for the next four months
whilst in Bessbrook Mill we put the finishing touches to the
written operational instruction. I was delighted to find that
Andrew Dudzinski had settled in quickly and was well on top of
his new job. A first class officer he had won the Sword of
Honour at Sandhurst but had recently returned from a
disappointing exchange appointment with the US Army's 82
Airborne Division. As a result he had resolved to leave the
Army in three months' time, and consequently was not popular
with the regiment's management. Clearly pleased that I had
placed my trust in him he was quite determined to give one
hundred per cent effort right up to his last day (which
unfortunately would come before the end of the tour), and so
go out on a high note.

The first few days of a battalion's tour and the last few days
of the outgoing battalion's are always a bit tense. There is
considerable over-crowding in every location, and most patrols
leaving the company bases consist of soldiers from the outgoing
unit led by, or reinforced by, officers and NCOs from the
incoming unit – a bit of a dog's breakfast. Yet the outgoing unit
retains total responsibility for the TAOR and it is therefore a
time for crossing fingers and avoiding irritation and
unnecessary friction.

To my surprise there were still two Spearhead Companies
attached to 1RS but this arrangement was due to end during
the following few weeks. Both of these came from 1st Battalion
The Green Howards and on the day of our arrival B Company
1 Green Howards was patrolling the border village of

Jonesborough when terrorists opened fire on them from the hill across in the South which dominates the village. Fire was returned and in the ensuing fire fight two PIRA terrorists were thought to be injured. This claim was confirmed by the Garda (the Republic of Ireland's police force) the following day and they also disclosed that they had found some weapons. It was a rare success but what happened to the terrorists subsequently we never knew.

I spent a large slice of the evening talking to OC D Squadron 22 SAS and we discussed his tasks which were largely conceived in conjunction with RUC Special Branch. The real potential of the SAS is in aggressive action for which they are painstakingly selected and trained to standards unequalled anywhere in the world, but such action is impossible in the absence of good intelligence so their efforts had to be directed towards improving our knowledge of certain suspected terrorists. He and I had struck up a reasonable relationship which was qualified by the natural reluctance of anyone in the SAS to confide and place their trust in an outsider (ie: one who had not passed the SAS selection course and so become a member of their club).

The following day I went round the patch to visit each of the company bases and the Newry RUC Station. Everything seemed well under control and my advance party appeared to be raring to go and anxious for the arrival of the main body. In the evening I attended Philip Davies' daily briefing session which was a regular feature of life at 17.30 each day at Bessbrook Mill. It provided an excellent opportunity to check over the events planned for the following day and to update the CO on what had occurred during the current day. I found it extremely valuable and resolved to continue the idea when we were running the show.

Tuesday 13th April was a day of conferences as was every succeeding Tuesday. The first was at 10.00, the District Action Committee (DAC). Membership of this group fell solely to members of the Security Forces (RUC and Army) and all those with a finger in the RUC's H Division were expected to attend. The division's Chief Superintendent and the CO of the South Armagh battalion were joint chairmen (this curious arrangement was symbolic of the Army's reluctance to support wholeheartedly police primacy), and others who attended were the COs of 2 UDR and 3 UDR, and the Newry RUC Superintendent. Not a lot was achieved at this meeting except that, and this was important, it was an opportunity for the RUC and the Army to get together, for without the discipline of a weekly meeting some who attended and didn't have daily contact with the other parties, were likely to get a bit out of touch.

The second meeting, and also a weekly event, was what we call in the Army an Orders Group (O Group). Normally O Groups are somewhat one-sided, that is at battalion level the CO telling his subordinates what is required of them and their companies. However, I was keen to develop my O Groups in Ulster into two-way sessions, so although there was a strong element of my telling my subordinates what was required, I did want to get feed back from them and to cross fertilise ideas between companies. Members of the O Group arrived in time for lunch because it was very much part of the deal that the company commanders coming in from their bases could have one moderately civilised meal a week. However, lest the reader gets the wrong impression, this was not a well lubricated lunch – like everyone in the battalion we were pledged to virtual abstinence for the whole of the tour.

The last meeting of the day was that of the Local Security Committee (LSC) which was being held for the very first time at Bessbrook Mill (usually it was held elsewhere in the District Council's area). Maybe it was the novelty of the venue, but there was an exceptionally good attendance; the chairman and vice-chairman of Newry and Mourne District Council, several councillors, and representation from the Northern Ireland Office (the office of the British Secretary of State) and the RUC. A number of councillors took the opportunity to 'bend my ear'. The gist of their message was simple – some patrolling tactics and any harassment of the local population can be totally counter-productive. None of this was surprising and again like the DAC meeting, not a lot of business was transacted, but it was a valuable opportunity to exchange views with local politicians, and most especially for them to voice their disquiet about Security Force activities.

Wednesday, 14th April, was the last day before we assumed responsibility for the TAOR. It was a quiet, relaxing day when I could reflect on why we were in South Armagh. The Army of course was in Northern Ireland in some strength simply because the RUC and their part-time back-up, the B Specials, had become overwhelmed during the Civil Rights Riots of 1969/70. The behaviour of the B Specials was very questionable although in fairness to them they were neither equipped nor trained to deal with rioters. Nevertheless they were disbanded as a force, the RUC was disarmed (it had always been an armed police force) and many full-time RUC officers left in disillusionment and disgust. The result was a very small dispirited rump of the RUC which needed total reconstruction, retraining and enlarging before it could begin to uphold law and order again in the Province.

Whilst the RUC was sorting itself out the Army was left holding the law and order 'baby' alone in many parts of Northern Ireland, especially the staunch Catholic areas. Throughout this period terrorism grew and with hindsight it can be seen that many of the decisions taken by the Army and Government served only to assist PIRA recruitment. In the space of two years the Army went from being welcomed as saviours of the Catholic population in 1969 to being loathed as an army of occupation by the early 1970s. By 1976 we had at last reached a state when the re-armed RUC had gained enough confidence and strength to once more resume the correct position in our democracy of the civil power leading with the Army in support. This was then and still is known as police primacy.

The RUC's first steps in this new situation were very tentative and none more so than in South Armagh. Many RUC policemen had been recruited recently and knew only the situation in which they were armed and in which when they wished to patrol Catholic areas they could do so only within the umbrella of support from the Army. This was compounded in South Armagh by the situation in which none of the RUC policemen knew the area because of course they were from elsewhere in the Province and invariably Protestants; certainly there was no question of South Armagh Catholics volunteering to join the force.

Policemen therefore were posted to the border RUC stations from the eastern part of Northern Ireland on tours of up to a year. They lived and slept at the stations which they reached in Army helicopters, visiting their homes only on their rest days. In South Armagh's most Nationalist areas, that is the area to the south and west of Newry, they saw themselves therefore very much in hostile territory and were apprehensive (with considerable justification) of leaving the sanctuary of their police stations which the Army guarded for them. There was one exception to this which was the mobile Special Patrol Group (SPG) which desperately wanted to patrol by car into South Armagh but the Chief Superintendent and I considered that their sorties would probably only serve to aggravate an already tricky situation, so we forbade them entry to that most hardline area. This saved us from a lot of unwarranted irritation and them from unnecessary fatalities.

It is always worth reflecting why South Armagh is so anti-British and difficult. Going back to the creation of the state of Northern Ireland in 1921 there was considerable debate about where the border should run between North and South. The old Irish province of Ulster consisted of nine counties but in the end only six (Fermanagh, Tyrone, Londonderry, Antrim, Down and Armagh) were incorporated into the North (had the other three been included Northern Ireland's permanent Protestant majority would have been reversed). The people residing between Newry and the border felt very strongly that as an almost totally Catholic grouping, they were on the wrong side of the line and attempts were made (the 1924 boundary commission) without success, to have the border adjusted.

Policing this area was a tenuous arrangement from the start. Many local inhabitants took advantage of the border and the resultant price differentials between Northern Ireland and Eire. Smuggling, animals particularly, became a normal behaviour pattern. The RUC 'policed' the area from the RUC 'barracks' in the principal villages and small towns but the local RUC sergeants and constables had to exist within the community so a 'blind eye' was usually turned to the more harmless pursuits of the inhabitants. Many of these were farmers with very large families but just a few acres of pasture (rarely more than twenty) where they grazed a few bullocks, kept a cow or two, reared pigs and a full range of domestic animals (dogs, cats and chickens). Their single storey whitewashed farmhouses were tiny and the families lived in primitive squalor in one or two rooms. Many of the sons of such families were 'unemployed', that is they drew benefits from the benevolent British Government, and it was natural that they would turn their minds to some means of creating an additional (untaxable) income outside farming.

So in South Armagh proper, and by this I mean the area south of a line drawn due west to the border from Newry, 'normality' in the law and order sense was something quite apart from 'normality' in the remainder of Northern Ireland or the United Kingdom. Many of the people of South Armagh, and their associates immediately across the border, were a tightly knit and interbred group of lawbreakers. They were used to helping each other on a daily basis and warning of the presence of the foreigner – the RUC or Customs and Excise men. In 1970, therefore, it was quite natural that they should take to terrorism like ducks to water. Their PIRA group is easily the most successful in the Province, and they have killed or seriously injured a very large number of soldiers and policemen without suffering much attrition themselves. Their knowledge of the countryside is of course intimate and detailed, especially when compared with that of constantly changing Army and RUC personnel many of whom are city dwellers with no empathy for the countryside.

The South Armagh PIRA were in the happy position that they could repeat their pattern of attacks against a succession of new arrivals confident in the near certainty that they were always one step ahead and held the initiative. The nearness of the 'sanctuary' of the Republic was a potent fact in their planning. Many of their attacks were actually conducted from the South in the sure knowledge that the British Army was forbidden from crossing the border, and even when they were fully in Northern Ireland no place in South Armagh is further than seven minutes' driving time from the border, and most of it is within two minutes.

In this situation the Army's role was to attempt to achieve three objectives; reassurance, deterrence and attrition. These led to our day to day activities which were to go on relentlessly for the next four months and I will try to describe the conflicting demands here in outline. As previously mentioned the Army bases had generally grown around the old RUC 'barracks' which had been built originally to accommodate a handful of RUC men but had been expanded since 1969 by ad hoc building to accommodate well over a hundred men in dreadfully cramped conditions. These 'barracks', and particularly those at Forkill and Crossmaglen were marooned in a sea of Republican (Catholic) discontent. The RUC were present in very small numbers and could not normally contemplate going out to 'police' the area without a large Army patrol in attendance. So to the RUC officers posted to these RUC stations, the Army provided total reassurance for without their presence there could have been no police activity at all.

In 1976 the first steps were being taken to reintroduce the RUC to the local population. Some RUC officers were very afraid and both RUC and Army found the joint patrols unusual to say the least. Naturally the Army also brought reassurance to the Protestants in the area, but there were very few of them and they tended to be grouped in small enclaves on the edges of South Armagh proper. To the Catholics of course the Army was not reassuring at all. They saw the British Army as an Army of occupation – a foreign power holding down their (Irish) homeland by force of arms, and it was difficult for the Army to avoid giving substance to these sentiments.

Each RUC station had to be guarded, and to prevent or deter terrorists from attacking the stations, especially with mortars, the local area had to be patrolled. If this patrolling was on a continuous basis it consumed a large number of men who were not therefore available for other more productive tasks; and if it was too infrequent the terrorists were given ample opportunity to attack. Abandoning the border RUC stations, Forkill and Crossmaglen especially had been discussed with the Army in 1973 but rejected. Certainly it made sense to many of the more thoughtful members of the Security Forces at the time, but reaction from the hardline Loyalists would unquestionably have been adverse. In practice abandonment would have enabled us to base ourselves at Bessbrook and to spend more time on offensive patrolling and less time on defensive patrolling. Such military logic would have found few supporters amongst the 'not an inch' Unionists so we remained in the border stations at great cost to human life. All movement into and out of them is either on foot or by helicopter, and the local population is perfectly placed to monitor each patrol which enters or leaves a base. As in so many things a compromise has to be struck. Inevitably, however, local defensive patrols to deter terrorist attacks on a base are seen by the local inhabitants as a somewhat overbearing military presence and this is bound to be. Who anywhere would welcome being stopped and searched on their way home after seeing their girlfriend, or how many young mothers would be happy to have their prams searched and their babies disturbed?

Another variety of deterrent patrolling is away from the base to discourage terrorists from setting up landmines, booby traps, shooting incidents and the like. In South Armagh particularly these have always been directed solely against members of the Security Forces, so the very act of patrolling the countryside to deter provides the Heaven-sent opportunity which the terrorist seeks to take advantage of.

Theoretically if we stopped patrolling there would be no incidents – that is no terrorism. But it is not that simple. In South Armagh an absence of patrols would mean that terrorists would have a free hand to terrorise and murder the few remaining Protestants; freedom to carry out their smuggling unhindered; and freedom to take their terrorism further into the hinterland. Worse, it would give the terrorists ample opportunity to set up complicated traps into which they would try to lure Security Forces, for above all they need to kill soldiers and policemen in order to heighten the tension, to reinforce their grip on the population and in the process achieve the publicity without which every terrorist organisation would die. Over the years these lure incidents (hi-jacks, kidnapping, telephone calls, information received) have successfully attracted the Security Forces into areas where they can be killed and all too often this is exactly what has occurred. Consequently a complex cat and mouse game has developed with, sadly, the PIRA invariably holding the initiative and the Security Forces playing the mouse.

In South Armagh many of us considered that the most profitable activity for the Security Force patrols is to lie still and watch what is going on; to see and not be seen. Even this is more easily said than done because the very act of getting into a position unobserved is complex even at night, particularly given the smallness of each farm, the animosity of the population, and their natural curiosity and familiarity with their own surroundings. So deterrence is a tricky concept. To the outsider, the more troops there are on the ground the more simple it is to deter or prevent terrorism, but that is only true if there are so many troops that nothing can move at all. Short of that figure, which for many practical reasons is quite unobtainable except for short periods in tiny areas, all the additional troops do is, somewhat perversely, help the terrorist. The natural reaction which we have seen over the years to a rise in incidents in a particular area of Ulster is to increase the force level, but often as not all it actually achieves is an increase in the number of potential targets thus making the terrorists' task easier, not more difficult.

In summary, a paucity of Security Forces pleases the Catholic (Nationalist) population, worries the Protestants (Unionists), makes life easy for the terrorists but more difficult for them to kill and get publicity; an abundance of Security Forces annoys the Catholics, pleases the Protestants, makes life more difficult for terrorists but easier for them to conduct successful operations. Logically, therefore, the less the Army patrols South Armagh the more content will be the population (it being almost wholly Catholic), and the number of fatal incidents will fall. It is an argument which is difficult to fault but it runs diametrically against one's military instincts. The compromise is to patrol incessantly, but in low profile spending most of the time invisible and static.

Finally, attrition. Spotting a terrorist is an extremely time-consuming and laborious business. Terrorists are just ordinary men (and women) living within the community who very occasionally do something to help the PIRA cause. The principals, the organisers and terrorists of the South Armagh PIRA gang, rarely exceed about twenty in number but they can count on the active or tacit support of a fair number of others. If the terrorist went about wearing a uniform, masked his face and carried a weapon every terrorist in Ireland would have been put behind bars or killed many years ago, but PIRA terrorists are not like that. Those who have custody of weapons or explosive hide them somewhere where they can easily get at them but where direct association cannot be proved. For those living in South Armagh and the immediate area to the South (Counties Monaghan and Louth) this is very simple to achieve as the border can be worked to the advantage of terrorists on both sides of it. Catching terrorists 'red-handed' is extremely difficult to achieve, and of course shooting at them, given the constraints of the law, is an even less likely occurrence.

This may seem a difficult statement to accept given the resources, sophisticated equipment, and manpower at the disposal of the Security Forces, but a simple example will serve to illustrate some of the ways in which the dice become loaded in the terrorist's favour. Let us suppose that a terrorist gang has decided to set up a bomb ambush to be triggered by electrical detonation when a patrol passes. The plan may be made weeks, even months ahead and a suitable site selected. The virtues of a good site are that the bomb (which may consist of several large containers) can be rapidly concealed, that a patrol is likely to pass the chosen spot or can be lured there, and that the firing point is either in the Republic or within a very short travelling time of it. South Armagh contains literally hundreds of sites which match these criteria.

In its simplest form a bomb (or improvised explosive device – IED) consists of three components; the main bulk of the explosive which determines the power of the explosion, a detonator, and a booster. The detonator alone is not powerful enough to set off the main charge so a booster of slightly more volatile material than the main charge must be added. Stealing all three of these items is quite possible but commercial sources (mainly quarries) have tightened up on their procedures and of course theft is against the law. So the terrorists have learnt to manufacture home-made substitutes which are easily mixed, effective and less likely to bring them to the notice of the police. In addition as a bonus detonators, and relatively small quantities of commercial explosive are sometimes available through international arms dealers.

Detonators are usually electric, that is they explode when a tiny electric current is passed through them. This can be arranged by connecting them by wire to a battery, which is a good safe distance away, or by placing a radio receiver and small battery alongside the IED so that on receipt of the firing signal the circuit to fire the detonator is completed. Immediately the advantage of radio control is apparent, there being no physical connection between the IED and the firer, the positioning of both can be more flexible. On the other hand the radio control variety requires complicated circuitry to ensure that the device explodes when the terrorist wants, and not in response to other extraneous signals in the ether.

Manufacture of the main explosive charge can take place anywhere but for the South Armagh PIRA it has been traditionally done in the South. The basic ingredient being agricultural fertiliser, the mixing process is very easy to conceal in a predominately farming community. Once made, the IED is either moved immediately to the ambush site or more usually hidden in a non-attributable spot until required.

If the device is to be triggered by electric current, a length of cheap household wire must be laid between the bombsite and the intended firing point. This can be completed at any time, even months before it will be used, and is often carried out most skilfully by making excellent use of the contours of ditches, walls and hedges. The advantage of laying the wire well ahead is that it allows time for it to blend in completely with the surroundings as the vegetation grows up.

The point in the operation when the gang is most at risk is when they are moving and emplacing the device. First they need to be certain that there are no Security Force VCP's around so naturally the shorter the distance over which they have to move it the easier life is, and they must be certain that there are no patrols in positions from where they might spot suspicious activity. Often the chosen site for the bomb will be a culvert, ditch or hedgerow where concealment will be relatively straightforward, but in any event the site will have been made ready so that positioning, connecting up any wiring and concealment can be completed rapidly. Often this will be done at night.

Once the bomb is in position the rest is straightforward. All those engaged in the plot thus far are almost completely free of all association, the only person at any sort of risk is the volunteer chosen to spring the ambush. This volunteer will frequently be a youth anxious to make his mark with the gang and to earn their respect and recognition. But even he is unlikely to get caught, and if he does he is not committing an offence unless he is literally caught with his finger (or finger prints) on the firing button. Given the fact that after an explosion everyone, no matter how well trained, takes a few moments to collect his thoughts the volunteer can use this pause to make good his exit or certainly distance himself far enough from the scene as to make proof of involvement extremely difficult to make in court.

So over the years our (Security Force) attrition of the South Armagh PIRA has been very poor whereas theirs of us has been quite significant. In a way this is hardly surprising as we help them by moving around in easily identifiable uniformed groups, in obvious helicopters and from known bases. For the terrorist to monitor our movements is literally child's play and is often carried out by children; unfortunately the reverse is not true. Of course, deterrence and attrition could much more easily be achieved if democratic principles were ignored. This is what the hardline Unionists would like but their union is with Great Britain and that union – the United Kingdom – eschews, quite rightly, all trappings of the totalitarian state.

The remainder of the battalion was due to arrive, under Edward Gardener, the following morning having sailed overnight across the Irish Sea. Thursday, 15th April I thought, would be a busy and long day so I went to bed early to wake to a spring morning that was immaculately bright and sunny. Few places look more beautiful than South Armagh in sunlight. Everything worked like clockwork and three of my companies were complete in their bases by 10.00, so we effected the handover and at 10.07 precisely 3 PARA became responsible for providing support to the RUC in South Armagh. B Company was still missing but they eventually arrived at 11.30. It turned out to be a busier day than I had anticipated – so much so that I wrote very little in my diary – two or three words serving to remind me of some fairly interesting incidents.

# CHAPTER FOUR

# A Dramatic Beginning

## *15th-21st April 1976*

The first four events of the day were very straightforward and somewhat typical. The planned clearance of an IED on the Dublin to Belfast railway line at a point just north of the border turned out to be a non-event; the 'bomb' was in fact a hoax. (Regrettably though, a hoax takes as much time, effort, caution and nervous energy to clear as does a real bomb, and of course it is a lot less risky for the terrorist to set up.) Shots were heard south of Crossmaglen, almost certainly in the Republic. An abortive attempt was made to hi-jack a lorry on the Concession Road (this is the road south-west of Crossmaglen which although running through Northern Ireland connects two Southern Irish towns, Dundalk and Castleblaney). In the fourth incident, £4,000 was stolen from the Newry main post office by armed robbers – the money possibly, though not necessarily, going to fund PIRA activities. The fifth incident was a classic 'own goal' when a Royal Military Police car returning to Portadown crashed, quite seriously injuring two soldiers.

But it was two further incidents which were completely unique and somewhat unexpected. The first of these occurred at 19.45 when a RAF Wessex helicopter, which was just about to touch down on the landing site (LS) at Crossmaglen, was fired upon by several automatic weapons and an RPG7 (the Soviet shoulder launched anti-tank weapon). It suffered superficial damage, notably a fractured fuel line and landed safely. The crew, who were the only people aboard, scampered quickly into the base shaken but none the worse for the experience. The LS at Crossmaglen at that time was just outside the perimeter fence of the base on the edge of the Gaelic Football pitch.

Overlooked by the new housing estate just off Dundalk Road on the opposite side of the pitch, the fact that it was where it was had been a bone of contention with the locals ever since it became established there. The suspected and actual firing points as can be seen from the map opposite, gave all the advantage to the terrorists. The direct route to it from the base was dreadfully exposed across open ground, whereas the terrorists' withdrawal route to the Dundalk Road, and thence to the border less than 60 seconds away by vehicle, was nicely concealed.

'A' Company's quick reaction force (QRF), prepared for just such eventualities but not expecting any action so early in the tour, reacted very positively. 240 rounds were fired at the points from which the ambush was thought to be mounted (the under construction housing estate on the opposite side of the football pitch), and five men were arrested and handed over to the RUC. It was no surprise that none of these turned out to be actively involved in the ambush and that no empty cases were found in the area of the supposed firing point. Indeed it was not until four days later that a patrol searching the village hall quite close to the LS discovered 51 empty cases which were, we presumed, at the site of the actual firing point. In any event the culprits and the weapons would have sped across the border almost before the helicopter had flopped onto the LS.

The incident was particularly interesting in that it was the first time that a RAF Wessex helicopter had been successfully shot at and the first time that an RPG7 had been used against a helicopter so far as we were aware. It also illustrated vividly just how difficult it is to identify the source of shooting, especially in an urban area. For the PIRA the ambush was a failure for there was no publicity and because the aircraft was quickly patched up, enough for it to limp back to Bessbrook, they must have assumed that they had missed their target. For us, however, it pointed up what we had known for many years, that helicopters landing and taking off from the border bases were very vulnerable.

I took the opportunity to go out to visit Colin Thomson at Crossmaglen. I found everyone there in good heart and the incident had certainly got their adrenalin flowing. I spent some time chatting with the soldiers and it was not until about 23.15,

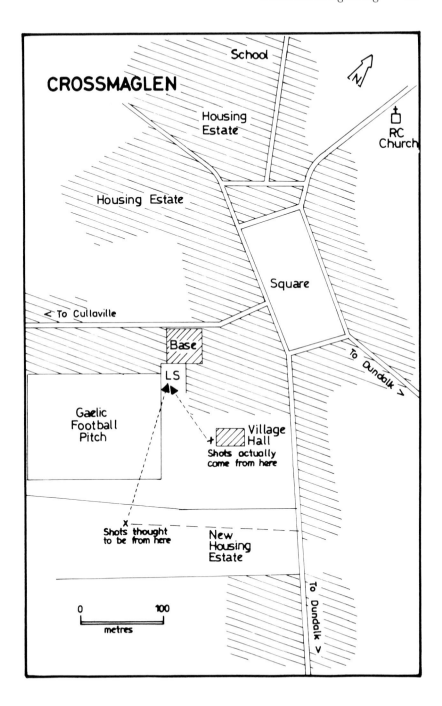

CROSSMAGLEN

School

Housing Estate

RC Church

Housing Estate

Square

< To Cullaville

Base

LS

To Dundalk ˅

Gaelic Football Pitch

Village Hall

Shots actually come from here

x
Shots thought to be from here

New Housing Estate

To Dundalk ˅

0          100
metres

when it was quite dark, that we took off from Crossmaglen to return to Bessbrook. The Wessex had already flown away and the few lights of the little market town winked invitingly below as we gained height, effectively cloaking the hatred and hostility of the earlier events. As we turned for 'home' the lights of Castleblaney and Dundalk seemed very near and almost enticing, emphasising if emphasis were needed, just how close those towns are to South Armagh. Settling on course for Bessbrook the glow of Newry beckoned ahead. During the journey of about ten minutes I chatted to the pilot and listened to the almost lifeless battalion command radio net. Suddenly that silence was broken by an SAS patrol which said cryptically 'have a bodybag waiting on the LS for us when we arrive'. This was an electrifying transmission but I was not in the business of asking my HQ on the radio what was happening – I was too conscious that many ears could be monitoring our conversation which would have carried many miles from the height of a helicopter. But on arrival at Bessbrook I was naturally more than keen to find out what the message meant. I had not to wait long for on the Bessbrook LS, which is fully capable of taking at least six helicopters, was a small reception committee from the SAS squadron headed by the squadron commander. Not long afterwards another helicopter landed with on board a four man SAS uniformed patrol and the dead body of one Peter Joseph Cleary, aged 25 of Belleek.

The story was quite simple. The patrol had been tasked with watching a house south of Forkill just 50 metres from Southern Ireland where Cleary, a wanted man, was expected to attend a party at the house of his girlfriend whom he was due to marry later in the month. Having made a positive identification at about 21.30, the patrol decided to move in on the house and arrest Cleary. This they did and they then escorted him to a nearby field. At about 22.20 they requested a helicopter to pick them up, but because they wanted it to land so close to the border permission had first to be obtained from Brigade HQ. Whilst waiting one man, armed with a rifle, was left guarding Cleary whilst the other three members of the patrol prepared to signal by torch to the expected helicopter and to guard the LS, for they were in a very vulnerable situation. Sometime around 23.25, and as the helicopter came in to land in the dark,

Cleary attempted to attack the SAS man guarding him. He was shot in the chest and killed in self-defence from a distance of about four feet. Permission to fly had not been given until 23.15 so by the time the helicopter had got there and back it was about 23.40 when the party touched down at Bessbrook with Cleary's body.

The question then was what to do. I immediately asked for the RUC Division Chief Superintendent and the RMP Special Investigation Branch (SIB) both of whom arrived quite quickly. Having established that neither Cleary's relatives nor his girlfriend were aware of his death, I quickly determined, supported when he arrived by the Chief Superintendent, that we would delay releasing the news of his death or the body to the local Daisyhill Hospital, Newry for a few hours. This would ensure that the story of his death would be too late for the latest editions of the local and national newspapers, and would also pretty well guarantee that when we did release a press statement it could be both accurate and comprehensive. Most important, our account would be the first to be received by the media. In the event the body was removed from Bessbrook by the RUC at 03.25, and the next of kin were informed by their parish priest shortly afterwards.

By getting our considered statement to the press before the PIRA 'disinformation' machine could concoct theirs, we achieved quite excellently accurate reports on the early morning radio programmes and later in the day on TV. Newspaper coverage was naturally light as the incident had ceased to be newsworthy by the time they went to press late on 16th April. Inevitably there was subsequently some speculative comment, triggered by the PIRA accusation of 'cold-blooded murder' by the SAS, but as their version of the story was out much later than ours, it was ours which was accepted by all except the most partisan.

Support for the SAS was solid throughout the Army and RUC and it was quite clear, even at this early stage, that the man who fired the shot would be backed up wholeheartedly by all branches of the Civil Authority. This was as it should be; the soldier had acted in accordance with the Army's Yellow Card which permits firing with or without warning 'if there is no other way to protect yourself, or those whom it is your duty to protect, from the danger of being killed'. As he faced the inevitable questioning and efforts by the PIRA propaganda machine to blacken his name, it must have been a considerable comfort to know that he had acted within the law.

The death of Peter Cleary was the first big controversy involving the SAS since their deployment into South Armagh was formally announced earlier in the year in the wake of the spate of sectarian killings. It was certainly a pity that the first occasion on which a terrorist was killed by the SAS was not more clear cut; the ideal would have been to shoot an armed terrorist. However, the incident served two very useful purposes, it showed the terrorists that they ought not to trifle with the SAS's determination and skill (had Cleary not tried to take advantage of the dark and the distraction of the arriving helicopter to overpower his solitary guard he would be alive today), but it also taught them (if they needed further encouragement) to be really frightened of the SAS. Believing their own propaganda, the PIRA was quite convinced that Cleary was cold-bloodedly murdered and later claimed him as one of their 'staff captains' (a euphemism for an active terrorist). Undoubtedly Cleary was the right man and the Province was well rid of him, for the RUC had, so I was informed at the time, evidence to implicate him in several serious crimes.

Naturally the man who shot Cleary was questioned extensively by both the RUC and the RMP SIB which resulted in him being placed under a very considerable strain. In due course the Director of Public Prosecution reviewed the case and the soldier was brought to trial for doing his duty, such is the heavy price of our brand of democracy. Thankfully he was acquitted.

Few people outside the more specialist elements of the Army can begin to imagine the high tension in that field, so near to the border, on the night of 15th April. The patrol had been hiding close to the target house for a number of days. Having been dropped some distance away at night they had then made their way to their chosen hiding places before dawn. Ideally all four men should have stuck together but the only spot which gave a good view of the house was so restricted that only two men could safely occupy it, and the other two found they were forced to use a hide several hundred metres away. Not only did they have to keep a constant watch on the house but they had to look to their own safety. Local farmers using dogs walked their hedgerows daily and any telltale could alert the farmer who would quickly inform the PIRA. Many such covert OPs have been attacked by PIRA over the years, consequently extreme caution was the order of the day. Eating, washing and defecating were virtually ruled out, and sleep which would have been easily taken if all four men had been together was not possible. After living like this, they were obviously delighted to identify, move in on and capture their subject, Cleary. For them the waiting was over and they expected to be whisked quickly back to Bessbrook, but instead they had what must have seemed an interminable wait. Had Cleary realised the strain under which these young men were operating I feel certain that he would have been less foolhardy.

So ended my first day responsible for military support in South Armagh. As I went to bed at about 03.00 I reflected that if they were all like that, we would have an interesting tour. I woke early after a restless night. The combination of an unfamiliar bed and a lot of noise outside, had conspired together to keep me awake for much of what remained of the short night. Consequently when I went to my Operations Room at 07.30 to find it filthy and a number of the routine tasks still incomplete I was not best pleased. My short temper did at least have the effect of ensuring that for the next four months it was invariably immaculate.

That second day was very quiet, a few unidentified shots, a hoax, and a small find. At 12.15 a BBC TV team visited the scene of Cleary's arrest and death as did a team from the RUC and at 19.30 a crowd of about 200 arrived at the Daisyhill Hospital to escort Cleary's body to his home village of Belleek. About 50 of the men dressed in para-military uniforms and black berets (many of whom we photographed clandestinely) escorted the coffin which was covered in a Republican tricolour, proof if any were finally needed that Cleary was an important member of the PIRA. His funeral, we learnt, was to be in Belleek on Easter Monday and I started to give the matter some thought because terrorist funerals are not an everyday event in South Armagh; indeed it would be more accurate to compare them with snow in the desert. It seemed that I was being presented with a unique opportunity to find out who supported or were members of the PIRA, and I was determined not to pass it up.

A more immediate problem though was dealing with the over-reaction by HQ Northern Ireland (HQNI) to the Wessex incident. Without any consultation they imposed a restriction on the number of helicopters which could remain on the ground overnight at Bessbrook, and this immediately reduced our ability to respond to an incident, and wasted fuel and aircraft flying hours ferrying back and forth to Aldergrove. Even less reasonable was a proposal that every RAF Wessex or Puma flight should be accompanied by an Army Gazelle (which was unarmed). Luckily I was able to scotch the second idea which was just plain silly and I wrote in my diary that night, 'There is quite evidently too much influence by HQNI on what happens at battalion level.' The fact is that the Army is extremely adept at shutting stable doors, but usually after the horse has bolted.

However, I was more concerned with commanding 3 PARA than becoming involved in futile arguments with HQNI. I visited every company and HMS *Alert* and I was pleased that Joe Baker's company had a good find of two pistols in the Derrybeg Estate in Newry. These were found abandoned in the middle of the road when a car was surprised by a patrol. Apparently the inhabitants were in the process of moving them, or were just getting nervous. Either way it was a good sign.

Having thought about Cleary's funeral I decided it was too good an opportunity to ignore, to search and check all those who attended. I anticipated that some of the mourners would have handguns (shots over the coffin was a standard PIRA rite), but I also knew that to interfere with the funeral itself would cause a riot, which we had insufficient manpower to deal with ourselves. I therefore decided, with the Chief Superin-tendent's concurrence, to check everyone as they left the funeral and I briefed Andrew Dudzinski along these lines and left him to plan the operation in detail.

The following day was Easter Sunday; it was also my wedding

anniversary. Traditionally Easter in Northern Ireland is a day of marches and this Easter was no exception. Several were held and I went to watch the two planned for Newry. The first was organised by PIRA who marched to the cemetery where they were harangued by someone neither we nor the RUC recognised. They just managed to get away before the second march, organised by OIRA (Official IRA), arrived. Fine timing, but it was all very peaceful and provided us with a good opportunity to get covert video and still photographs of the participants.

After lunch I held an O Group for those involved in the Cleary funeral on the morrow. The plan in outline was very simple. A ring of covert OPs was to be established around the village during the night to act as eyes, and catchers of anyone who decided to break away across the fields. Five other groups would establish VCPs in and on the outskirts of the village once the funeral had started, so enabling us to check on everyone who had attended. No soldier or RUC officer would be visible until after the funeral service was under way.

On the Easter Monday the ritual started at Belleek at about 14.30 when the cortège moved off. Seen from a concealed OP on the hill overlooking the village, this was preceded by a colour party dressed in green berets, yellow masks and green anoraks carrying a furled tricolour. Between 50 and 75 women dressed in para-military uniforms were dotted amongst the crowd of about 800. As shots were fired over the grave and the funeral oration began my planned VCPs moved silently into position. Between 16.30 and 20.25 all departing cars were stopped and the occupants searched. Several houses where men and women dressed in para-military uniform were seen to enter were also searched as was the public house – Tully's Bar. There was no animosity and the locals took it all in good part.

It was interesting to note that very few of those attending came from Newry. Most were from the neighbouring villages and towns of Crossmaglen, Cullyhanna and Newtownhamilton or from the Republic. The result of the afternoon's work was a lot of names and photographs, and interestingly our first contact with one Liam Townson, later found guilty of the death of Captain Robert Nairac, who then and at the time of his death was working as a liaison officer with the RUC. Townson was the very last person to pass into the VCP on the road to Newtownhamilton and suspicious of him we arrested him for questioning, but after a few hours he was released.

Reading the Northern Ireland *Sunday News* that evening I noticed a short article entitled 'Why can't Bessbrook get a good night's sleep?' I reproduce most of it here as it accurately summed up life at the end of Bessbrook village closest to our Mill:

Women are going deaf, children are being dosed with valium and sleeping drugs and men are falling asleep at their work. That's the true life story of more than a dozen families living in the South Armagh village of Bessbrook.

It's all because of Britain's busiest heliport, built only yards from their back doors. For two years the families have watched and listened to helicopters landing and taking off from the pad as they carry troops and supplies in and out of the Army base at Bessbrook Mill.

At first it was almost a novelty but now the story has turned sour with frightening results. The unending clatter and roar of the chopper engines throughout the day and night has had such a devastating effect on the residents that even one four year old girl cannot get sleep at night without first taking a valium tablet and a sedative.

Most of the residents on the perimeter of the heliport are sleeping only with the help of drugs, mothers claim medical tests have proved that they are now partially deaf and one house which the helicopters repeatedly fly over has been shaken so often that cracks are snaking across the ceilings and walls.

'We have been trying to get this stopped for more than a year but it's only getting worse,' said the residents' spokesman, Mr Roy Black. 'It's like having helicopters landing in your back garden every five minutes. At times we have had as many as eight of them running their engines simultaneously. This house vibrates so much that even the sofa moves.' He pointed out that the residents beside the heliport – nicknamed locally as Bessbrook International – do not want to interfere with the security forces but the noise level was becoming so intolerable that they were considering moving out of the village.

Mothers who have to stay at home all day claim the noise has affected their hearing and doctors have told them that under no circumstances were they to leave their babies outside their houses in their prams. Windows have to be kept shut day and night, gardening for some has become impossible and one child has to leave her home each night to sleep in another part of the village.

Attempts by the villagers and South Armagh MP, Harold McCusker, to have the landing pad moved away from the houses have all failed.

I had considerable sympathy for the Bessbrook residents but we could not move our HLS and they could not move out of their houses. They had been given double glazing and other sound-proofing but as can be seen from the photographs (p.69) that could only be a palliative not a remedy.

Tuesday, the day of meetings, came and went with one incident typical of mindless Protestant terrorism in the shape of the Ulster Volunteer Force (UVF). They placed an IED on the railway line between Poynts Pass and Jerrats Pass (north of Newry) – 15 lbs of gelignite on a bridge over a canal. Had it gone off the result would have been quite disastrous and indiscriminate. I tried to use the incident as propaganda against the UVF but failed, Ulster TV news was not interested. The railway seemed to have a magnetic attraction for at 18.30 two men (this time obviously PIRA) tried to stop a train at Kilnasaggart Bridge (just north of the border) but they failed. Instead they just fired at the train and a helicopter which was overflying it. I had no doubt they had had a bomb ready for the train and I could expect it to be used somewhere else in the near future.

The following day I had planned a detailed tour of Newry with Joe Baker and we started early. It is an interesting town built on both sides of a valley so that even the worst council houses have lovely views. The town is split by the river which had been developed into a canal in more prosperous days and then fallen into disuse as industry and transportation methods were updated. Only four bridges crossed this canal which together with a one way circuit ensured that even the slightest obstruction would cause a monumental traffic jam, thus real bombs or hoax bombs in Newry could easily be used to bring the town to a standstill. There were also literally hundreds of ideal positions from which snipers could safely shoot at a military patrol sure in the knowledge that getting away was comparatively simple.

The Derrybeg council estate was quite the worst spot in Newry. A relatively modern estate rendered squalid by many of its inhabitants yet peppered with some excellent people who quite clearly took a tremendous pride in their houses and gardens. I felt very sorry for the last group. In many ways the Derrybeg is similar to several of the notorious Catholic estates in Belfast of which the Ballymurphy estate is the best known. All these estates are horrid, but largely because so many of the inhabitants have no standards and live in them like animals. To call it sub-standard housing is ludicrous, each house is solidly desirable, but these inhabitants could turn Eaton Square in Belgravia into a slum. The apocryphal story is of baths being used to store coal and I have actually seen that in Belfast. I have also seen a house occupied by a family of six in which there was not even a scrap of food other than a half bottle of milk, yet the parents went to the public house twice day.

Such thoughts were suddenly interrupted at 10.00 when I was summoned by radio to Brigade HQ. I arrived there at 10.30 to be told that an extra battalion was to be sent out from England on 24th June to look after the northern half of County Armagh, and in the process they would take over my bases at Newtownhamilton and Glenanne. However, the change was to be implemented more immediately and as an interim measure the 1st Battalion The Queen's Lancashire Regiment (1 QLR) – a resident regular battalion based at Ballykinler – would occupy the two bases I was to lose. I was not at all happy about the new plan because it committed the fundamental error of unnecessarily splitting the responsibility for supporting a police division between two units, as the Chief Superintendent, who till now had dealt only through me, would have to deal also with the CO of 1 QLR. I protested to the brigade commander but was quickly over-ruled and was sent off to inform my Chief Superintendent who having suffered the Army's deployments

**Above** *Night-time over the Mill.*

**Below** *Bessbrook village and Mill. The checkpoint at the entrance to the village is just below the base of the chimney hidden by the trees; the HLS is the fenced area at 4 o'clock of the chimney with the houses most affected by the noise at 3 o'clock.*

*The Derrybeg Estate, Newry.*

and re-deployments over the last several years was amazingly philosophical, indeed almost immune to the proposed change.

While I was with the Chief Superintendent we discussed our railway incidents and determined to try and crack the problem once and for all. He rang the chief railwayman in Dundalk who agreed to come up, and see us the next day.

The following morning I went first to see Ian Chapman at Newtownhamilton to explain the new deployment plans. He was very peeved about his company being brought back into Bessbrook; all company commanders naturally prefer the independence of running their own show so I tried to assure him that it would not be all bad, and I left him looking a bit more cheerful. Then to Forkill where Malcolm Cuthbertson seemed content. There I had the unpleasant task which came my way from time to time of holding 'orders' (the Army's version of a Magistrates Court). One soldier had accidentally fired his rifle and the automatic punishment for a 'negligent discharge' was a fine amounting to two weeks' pay. This was duly administered. As an aside here, I certainly could not have afforded to set a bad example (nor, incidentally, to lose two weeks' pay), consequently my pistol went unloaded for most of the tour.

So ended our first week in South Armagh; it had had its moments.

# CHAPTER FIVE

# A More Normal Week

## *22nd-30th April 1976*

Since August 1973 there had been about nine hi-jacking incidents involving trains and their crews on the line between Portadown and Dundalk. Most of these had occurred in the area between the border and Kileen bridge (about 1½ miles to the north). Naturally these hi-jackings attracted considerable publicity even in the mainland media and because the Army had to move cautiously to avoid booby traps on and off the train, it always gave the impression of being over-cautious and inept. IEDs, on the other hand, occurred much more frequently and because they involved neither hostages nor trains the publicity was minimal.

In December 1975 the Commander Land Forces (CLF) had had enough of the hi-jack egg on his face and he gave firm orders that hi-jackings were to cease and it was generally understood that he intended to make an example of any South Armagh battalion CO should he fail to comply with this order – certainly that is how it was explained to me by Philip Davies and the brigade commander.

Consequently a platoon with a minimum strength of twenty was continuously tied up patrolling on and around the railway. Inevitably called the 'railway children' it was an irksome business. They were required to stay out night and day and because their target was so linear, they were bound to set up patrolling patterns which invited PIRA retaliation no matter how hard they tried to ring the changes. Three whole pages of my Operation Instruction were devoted to the railway but in a nutshell the problem centred largely on the permanent way within two miles of the border. Most hi-jackings had occurred there and nearly all had involved northbound goods trains in the early morning or evening. Luckily these trains were infrequent for although it was the most important railway in Ireland only four passenger and four goods trains travelled in each direction on weekdays and at weekends there were no goods trains. Naturally our attention was focussed particularly on the goods trains and these were automatically overflown by a Scout helicopter (an onerous and expensive commitment). The effort to keep this little railway open in terms of men, money and risk was out of all proportion to its commercial value. Politically, however, it was probably significant.

At 15.00 on Thursday, 22nd April, with these thoughts in my mind I arrived at the Newry RUC station to meet the three railway officials from the South, one of whom was a Mr McArdle. They were a jolly group and we had an amicable and frank discussion. They were clearly impressed by the lengths to which we had to go to keep the line open, and I was relieved that they displayed at least some understanding of the risks we faced. In the middle of our talks, and as if to make the point, we learnt of yet another IED in the Kilnasaggart Bridge area (400 metres to the north of the border) – I mused that it was almost certainly the one that got away on Tuesday.

Mr McArdle and his team went away pledged to consider a range of options which included stopping passenger trains altogether, running trains in groups, increasing the number of permanent way men (they were very effective in patrolling the line because being civilians they were not in themselves targets), and even getting each passenger train to push a goods train in front of it (thus removing the danger to passengers from a bomb on their line whilst simultaneously giving the goods trains the protection of the passengers). However I was not at all hopeful that anything but an increase in the number of permanent way men would result.

After the Southerners had left I discussed with two Superintendents (the Deputy Divisional Commander and the Newry Town Superintendent) our plans for the Easter Uprising Diamond Jubilee Celebration which was due to be held in Dublin on the coming Sunday. As far as we knew many Republicans would be travelling from the North by both road and rail. If the railway remained open we would have to patrol it (which required manpower) yet we would not be able to check who was travelling as we did not usually board the trains because of the difficulty of getting on or off. After some soul searching therefore we decided to take the unusual step of closing the railway to force everyone onto the roads where we could mount a massive and comprehensive VCP operation. The closure was effected by the simple but unique ruse of declaring an IED on the line, a tactic not used before nor to my knowledge since.

The meeting over I went to Crossmaglen at 17.30 to see Colin. I decided to return by RAF Puma which proved a very exciting flight at low level, skimming and banking perilously around the hills and plunging stomach wrenchingly into the valleys with the aircraft's belly barely clearing the ground and the large rotor almost chopping the heather and leaves as we keeled over. Brilliant flying and perhaps even risky, but it did illustrate the differences in flying tactics between the Army and RAF. The RAF flew very low to reduce the risk of attack by surface to air missiles (SAM) (and of course it was exhilarating) but by so doing they made themselves more vulnerable to machine gun (MG) fire, to RPG 7s, and to power cables in poor visibility. The Army on the other hand flew high to avoid MG and RPG 7 fire on the basis that no SAM had so far been used by PIRA. My view was that the RAF had got it wrong, particularly as their low level routes between the border bases followed predictable paths quite regularly. I resolved to try to change their tactics for the passengers at risk in their aircraft were my soldiers.

Apart from helicopter my choice of conveyance for the tour would be limited by both regulation and common sense. Wearing civilian clothes I could use the hideously obvious blue Austin 1800 staff car either as a self drive or driven by Corporal Mitchum. In this mode we were obliged to carry pistols although the value of them should we encounter any terrorists was highly questionable, and we decided to put our faith in the accelerator if humanly possible. Alternatively for short trips it was quite customary to throw a civilian jacket or anorak over one's military clothing but clearly that would not defeat a cursory glance into the car. When I wished to go on a proper tactical patrol which would also involve an element of walking and contact with the public I used my rover group. This

**Above** *The railway, looking north from Kilnasaggart Bridge towards Newry. Moore's Bridge is centre frame.*

**Below** *The O'Meath VCP, sandwiched between the lock entrance to the Newry Canal from Carlingford Lough and the heavily wooded Flagstaff Hill*

consisted of two open landrovers each crewed by four (including myself) and fully armed (rifles and automatic weapons).

In making the decision about which mode to use time played an important part. It took at least ten minutes to extract my rover group crews from their proper employment so if time was of the utmost importance we used the car every time. The car, however, had a very poor radio so that whilst in the car I was to all intents and purposes out of contact with events. The rover group on the other hand had excellent communications and a professional signaller to maintain them. In a nutshell therefore the car was much more convenient but also much more risky and it was not long before the RUC were advising me that it had been compromised.

At 21.30 I went with my rover group down to Newry for a quick drive around. It was very peaceful indeed. But this was not the case everywhere, for at that very moment a patrol was being shot at at Mountainhouse (just west of Camlough). Two armed men had been seen in a car. A patrol went to investigate and three shots were fired at them. They returned nineteen rounds, claimed a possible hit and staked out the area all night ready for a detailed search the following morning. Unfortunately, as on so many occasions, this proved fruitless.

Friday, 23rd April, was very quiet. I attended the Brigade O Group at the old disused Knicker Factory in Lurgan, tied up arrangements for the weekend, and completed the final details for handing over Newtownhamilton and Glennane to 1 QLR. On my return to Bessbrook I found the General Officer Commanding, Lieutenant-General Sir David House, visiting. (Policy at that time was that senior officers could visit, even the company locations, without warning. This kept everyone on their toes and certainly did not concern me because I considered that my companies were usually in good order and open to scrutiny.)

After lunch the RUC Inspector in charge of the local SPG came to see me to request a free hand to patrol anywhere in South Armagh. I refused for the reasons that I had already thrashed out with the Chief Superintendent. (An anomaly of the SPG was that they were not responsible to the individual RUC divisions, rather they were under the area commander, in this case a charming and rather elderly Assistant Chief Constable. He was keen that they should patrol, but luckily he was not prepared to order my Chief Superintendent to comply and I was most thankful that in the RUC at least, the person responsible for an area had a fair amount of independence.)

On the subject of relationships with the RUC it is worthy of note that articles on Police Primacy or 'Ulsterisation' abounded in the Ulster and mainland press at that time. The main thrust was that Ulstermen (RUC and UDR) should take the brunt of enforcing law and order in the Province, leaving the Army free to fade into the background and to reduce its strength there. The complete withdrawal of the Army was not suggested, but reductions from the current strength of 14,000 to as little as 5,000 were openly mooted. Much of this talk was pretty fanciful but the principle of increasing the strengths and capabilities of the RUC and UDR whilst reducing that of the regular Army was absolutely sound and has continued steadily ever since. At its nadir eight years later the strength of the Army went below 9,000 although it sadly rose again in 1985, largely to counter over-reaction by extremists on both sides to the Anglo-Irish agreement. But in South Armagh despite the articles, the working parties, and the speculation, the Army continued more or less as before, except in Newry town where the RUC were able increasingly to adopt a higher profile.

Saturday is the day on which politicians traditionally hold their constituency clinics and Saturday, 24th April was clearly no exception as I was scheduled for visits by two prominent Unionist politicians. But the first news of the day was that, sadly, Andrew Dudzinski's father had died overnight, so I released him to see to the arrangements and attend the funeral.

The first politician arrived at 15.20 accompanied by a Captain Armstrong (an ex-member of the old Northern Ireland Convention). I noted in my diary that the politician did not impress me one little bit.

First he complained that someone he knew had had to stand at a VCP near Newtownhamilton for 2½ hours in his bare feet (a preposterous story). Then he quoted a doctor at Newtownhamilton as saying that the only time he had felt safe over the past 5 years was when 2 PARA were in charge in

1973 (I should have felt pleased because this is when I was last there, but I could not). All in all it was a most unproductive session and my general impression of him is that he is typical of that element in the Protestant community who are quite unable to see the other person's point of view. He advocated a policy of shoot on sight and damn the Yellow Card.

The second politician, Enoch Powell, arrived at 16.00, an intellectual giant in striking contrast to his Parliamentary colleague. His attitude was totally different and I enjoyed greatly the hour I spent in his company. Most perceptively he asked me what we thought we were doing in Newry and when I replied that we were producing an overt presence to instill confidence and at the same time were trying to root out terrorists especially from the council estates he asked if our presence was not counter-productive. He asked what would happen if the troops were withdrawn and suggested that people would feel more free to talk to the police. In posing this question he was, in my humble view, ahead of time. Neither the RUC nor the general public were ready then for such a step and it was not until four years later that the soldiers were withdrawn from Newry.

I replied that at the moment, many people felt more confident talking to soldiers than to the RUC, and that as information was in short supply yet was our life blood we could not risk having it cut off or further reduced. He also asked about the weapons we carried. Why, he wondered, did we have to carry rifles which were wholly inappropriate for carrying out a police function. I agreed, but pointed out that whilst PIRA had high velocity weapons it was essential to be able to match them in range and firepower. I gave the example of how a sniper at 300 metres would be totally confident to fire off a whole magazine if he thought that our only firearms were handguns. He took the point.

Our discussion ranged over the strength of the RUC and the efficiency of the SPG and UDR. I pointed out to him that unfortunately in the minds of the population of South Armagh these last two forces were associated irrevocably with Protestants and the B Specials. We discussed Army force levels and I explained that to achieve a position of no terrorist activity in South Armagh we would need about ten infantry battalions and excellent co-operation from the Republic. The current force level produced one soldier per square mile which was twice what we had in 1973, yet the level of activity was much the same. I tried to get across, I hoped successfully, that any further increase in force level short of my estimated ten battalions could well be counter-productive in that it would create more targets without there being enough to prevent terrorist activity. Pattern setting would be more obvious and the terrorist would need less patience.

At 18.00 another visitor, Brigadier Mervyn McCord, arrived. As overall commander of all eleven UDR battalions in the Province he was concerned that I was not giving those UDR units who were tasked to me at weekends interesting and challenging tasks and he was anxious that I should not treat them as second class citizens. He was right to be concerned for at their current state of training I did not trust the UDR, and neither did the Chief Superintendent. We had no intention of ever putting them to a task where they could let us or themselves down but I did not tell Brigadier McCord that, although I think he knew it.

After last light I went in my car, driven by Corporal Mitchum, to visit the VCPs on the two roads leading most directly to Dundalk and Dublin. In 1969 there had been a permanent Customs building just north of the border but it had been bombed out of existence early in the troubles and all that remained were the somewhat indistinct signs of its foundations. Since then a series of temporary caravans had been used by the Customs at different sites between Newry and the border, but all too often they had been destroyed by the Republicans. So the Dublin Road VCP had become a moving check point, always somewhere on the stretch of road but never in one place for too long. The other VCP was on the O'Meath road which ran alongside the canal and parallel to the Dublin Road. This VCP was a permanent building manned by half a platoon of my soldiers. It was well sited, in that it was difficult to attack, but it served very little useful purpose for it guarded a road which was little used; terrorists would naturally use roads which we did not guard, so by definition only innocents used the O'Meath crossing. At some time in the future I felt certain that an enterprising person would build an hotel on the site. However, for 3 PARA's tour, and for the foreseeable future, it was a white elephant which HQNI insisted that we had to occupy.

Having seen the two VCPs I returned to Newry to visit Support Company. Joe Baker was out but his intelligence officer was in so I was able to have a good talk with him. He was a very experienced fellow who had come up through the ranks. I had first encountered him in 1973 when I was commanding Support Company 2 PARA in the Ballymurphy Estate in Belfast and he was a colour-sergeant. He had an excellent grasp of covert work then and spent much of his time setting up OPs in derelict flats and houses from where he could acquire information on the movements of suspected terrorists either by observation or by eavesdropping. He was therefore a natural choice, now that he was an officer, to be the intelligence officer of Support Company 3 PARA. That evening he was very pleased with himself because he had acquired as much useful information in that first week as he had in the same place during two months in 1973.

I had arrived back in Bessbrook just as reports were coming in of a bomb which had apparently exploded at the Ulster Bar in Warrenpoint. This was clearly a UFV effort, no warning was given but luckily only one person was seriously injured. I decided to go down there and on my way I noticed a large column of smoke issuing from a factory in Newry. Irritatingly my car radio telephone was not working and as I was some distance from either the RUC station or Support Company I pressed on – wrongly with hindsight. For when I returned an hour later the area was a raging inferno which was well beyond the control of the local fire brigade. It transpired the following day that several Protestant-owned shops where the fire apparently started were also gutted.

Sunday dawned beautiful and bright. I flew around to look at the VCPs which were monitoring the minor road traffic to the Dublin celebrations. I did not see any, but was assured on the radio that they were all in position. The two principal VCPs I had visited the previous night were very busy, but there was no trouble and people were able to pass on their way quickly and in good humour.

It was such a nice day that in the afternoon I took my rover group, together with their ad hoc crews of drivers, clerks and the Regimental Sergeant Major, on a pleasant Sunday afternoon drive to the most peaceful part of the battalion area – Warrenpoint, Rostrevor and the hills to the north of them. It was so beautiful that it was easy to be lulled into thinking that Northern Ireland was also a peaceful and happy place. Clearly some of my patrols were feeling just this way, but not the PIRA. In the late afternoon a patrol led by Lieutenant Bill Edwards was fired upon near Meigh (north of Forkill) where they had a VCP but unfortunately they were unable to send a quick radio report which meant that the airborne reaction force (ARF) was not tasked in time and the culprits drove away without hindrance.

This is the first time that I have mentioned the ARF. We maintained at Bessbrook a Scout helicopter stripped of its doors and able to carry six men. They rested in a hut on the edge of 'Bessbrook International' where they were at immediate notice to respond to any incident which might occur in South Armagh, which meant remaining fully dressed with weapons and equipment ready to grab as they dashed to the helicopter. If the ARF was to be of any value at all it was imperative that it was 'scrambled' immediately an incident started; any delay was bound to ensure their arrival on the scene of an incident too late to be useful so the best policy was to get them airborne and then brief them by radio whilst they flew to the scene.

In the early evening a patrol from A Company came under fire in the area of Milltown, SE of Crossmaglen. They returned the fire, and the patrol commander evidently enjoyed himself because his patrol fired 250 fire rounds in response to the 80 fired at them. These two incidents highlighted the problems of soldiering in South Armagh; contacts were very brief, the initiative was always with the terrorist, and overt activities like VCPs in daylight were likely to occasion some riposte. I noted in my diary that night that 'what we want is dead terrorists, not empty cartridge cases'.

Monday, 26th April, was another beautiful day and a very quiet one. C Company cleared an IED which turned out to be nothing dangerous and work started at Newtownhamilton to demolish a number of derelict houses adjacent to the base to give more space and in particular enough for the erection of a new and much needed dining room. After lunch I had the honour to be visited at Bessbrook by Mr Airey Neave MP, Conservative Northern Ireland spokesman and a man with an enviable war record. Clearly a brave and mentally tough man he was smaller in build than I had anticipated. The SAS squadron commander and I briefed him and then answered his questions which were very straightforward. I thought afterwards that we had perhaps been too optimistic in predicting a real success in the not too distant future, but pessimism is a more regrettable sin. Our discussion over, I took him on a short helicopter trip around Newry and Carlingford Lough. He was an extremely affable but dynamic man who was destined to be fatally blown up by the Irish National Liberation Army (INLA) in 1979 at the House of Commons, only a short time before he could have become Secretary of State for Northern Ireland, a job for which he was being widely tipped at the time.

The following morning I was awoken shortly after 06.00 with the news that a car bomb had been reported on the Dublin Road to the RUC. Simultaneously patrols from Support Company and the RUC went to the scene. Captain Terry Lewis, the Support Company patrol commander, was reputedly cautious but nevertheless managed to drive past the bomb, which turned out to be in a parked Morris 1100. The RUC on the other hand knew the Morris 1100 was suspicious and committed the biggest blunder of all by rushing straight up to the car and pulling out some wires. ATO who had also been tasked, like Terry, drove in error straight past. Ludicrously, therefore, ATO and Terry's patrol finished to the south of the IED with the RUC and other rubber necks to the north. Eventually the device was defused by the ATO and the car was found to contain 200 lbs of home-made explosive and 20 lbs of Frangex.

The complete story behind the bomb was never properly unravelled but what seemed most likely was that the PIRA set up the car, together with its command wire, to catch an Army or RUC patrol. For some unexplained reason the bomb did not go off when they attempted to fire it so they telephoned the

RUC anonymously in order to get the bomb removed for it had become more dangerous to their supporters than their enemies. However, at the time neither we nor the RUC knew that, so we were very lucky that it was not just a simple booby trap. Had it been the RUC, and perhaps the Army also, would have suffered some fatalities.

At 17.30 a very old friend of mine, Lieutenant Colonel Peter Sincock, who was CO of 2nd Battalion The Royal Regiment of Fusiliers (2 RRF), visited Bessbrook. It was his battalion that was being sent out from England in June and he had come on a reconnaissance. After a quick briefing I took him to Newtown-hamilton and Glenanne by car to look round the two bases he would be occupying. Strictly speaking I was banned by HQNI rules from driving on those roads but in my view it was quite safe to do so once in a while. After supper we had a long chat about South Armagh and other things before retiring for an early night at just after midnight.

Wednesday, 28th April, dawned brilliantly again after a distinctly chilly night. My small room faced north and had huge impenetrable walls so the temperatures seemed to hover consistently at about 5°C lower than anywhere else in Bessbrook Mill. I had two senior visitors to look forward to that day, so first thing I flew to Crossmaglen and Forkill to make absolutely certain they were in good order. They were both immaculate and the men in both companies seemed very chirpy.

The first visitor was CLF, Major-General David Young. He was a Royal Scot and had a natural and deep affection for 1 RS the battalion 3 PARA had taken over from. Although we had been there nearly a fortnight this was his first visit to 3 PARA and I had not met him prior to that afternoon, but my impression then and thereafter was always that in his eyes we could never do as well in South Armagh as 1 RS had done. Nevertheless I noted that we had a useful meeting and he was most interested to find out what my plans were. I left him to go round my companies alone by helicopter whilst I looked after my second visitor, the Director of Military Operations (DMO) from the Ministry of Defence, I noted in my diary that:

he is clearly obsessed with electronic gadgetry – underground sensors and the like – which I am not very enthusiastic about, and I am concerned that this is unrealistic because he gives the impression that he expects his electronic devices to solve all problems when in my view this is somewhat fanciful.

I noted also that we mentioned to him our lack of absolutely reliable communications to our covert OPs and foot patrols in certain areas and he seemed to think that something could be done to improve matters.

At 16.30 someone fired a shot at the front sangar (the sandbagged sentry post) at Crossmaglen and the QRF quickly sped to the probable firing point in the neighbouring council estate. They entered a house to search it and whilst upstairs, Private Hastings accidentally fired his rifle which at the time he was resting muzzle down on his foot (an annoying habit). Luckily for him the bullet passed between his toes, but even more fortunate the bullet having passed through the floor to the room beneath narrowly missed some children sitting there. In the light of that incident it was hardly surprising that the fine for a 'negligent discharge' was two weeks' pay!

That evening I enjoyed a very pleasant working dinner in the Bessbrook Mess with Ian McCausland (3 UDR) and the CO of 22 SAS. I was just sliding off to bed early when at 23.45 I was summoned to the Operations Room. A Patrol Company patrol near the border close to the Dublin Road reported heavy firing to its south, and a Support Company patrol at Clontygora (a little to the east) reported heavy firing to its west. At the same time C Company lost contact with their platoon patrolling the railway so we suffered a fairly agonising fifteen minutes before contact was re-established with the platoon by helicopter radio relay (that is flying a helicopter to gain height and act as a mobile radio link).

Slowly it became clear that the Patrol Company patrol had been occupying an observation position (OP) very close to the border which during the day had been possibly discovered by a local farmer. Not wishing to take a chance, the experienced patrol commander, Sergeant Fenwick, had vacated the position immediately after last light to occupy a spot several hundred yards away. It was just as well he did, for the noise which was heard was a full blown attack on the empty OP. Some minutes after the attack the Support Company patrol saw two cars and several people arrive at two houses which were quickly surrounded and then searched, starting at 02.00. Nothing, unfortunately, was found.

At about this time a number of explosions were heard south of Crossmaglen, probably in the Republic (these were possibly mortar test firings). At first light a follow up search was carried out in the area of the vacated OP: 217 empty cases and 7 live rounds were found together with fragments of 3 pipe bombs (home-made grenades). At least four different calibre weapons had been fired.

After very little sleep I was up quite early on the 29th. By 10.00 the brigade commander, David Anderson, had arrived to give me a dressing down for having had a single four-man patrol so close to the border. This was strictly prohibited by him (his rule was a minimum of eight men), but he was really quite decent about my disregard of his orders. However, his meaning was quite clear – do not do it again. Before lunch I went down to the RUC station. There had been a few misunderstandings in the early hours of the morning with the HSB when we had wanted to search some houses in 'hot pursuit' (for which we needed his authority) and the message we got was that he was against this. It was the inevitable conflict of interest that is bound to occur from time to time. However, I poured oil on the waters and all was well until the next time.

After lunch I held my weekly O Group. I made eight points:

1. Minimum strength within 2000 metres of the border was to be eight men (two 4-man patrols) led by an officer or SNCO and if within 500 metres to be cleared by myself (in reality patrol strengths were most often twelve men).

2. Every patrol was to make sure it always had one leg on the ground in a good fire position.

3. The weather was nice but our men must not relax.

4. Every patrol was to be painstakingly briefed and debriefed and each weapon was to be check zeroed frequently.

5. At night when static, a high percentage of each patrol was to be alert (to this end patrols only carried sleeping bags at a scale of one between two).

6. Lost contact procedure was to be strictly adhered to and contact was to be established immediately there was any

shooting or explosions within earshot.

7. Patrols were to avoid setting predictable patterns, particularly in their use of helicopters.

8. We were using up too much of our luck.

Most of these points were simply re-emphasis of the Operational Instruction which I had issued at the beginning of the tour, but I thought that they were well worth repeating because they represented the keys to success, or failure. I was concerned about the radio communications in Malcolm Cuthbertson's company area. They were somewhat patchy and unreliable. Inevitably, as on the previous night, it caused unnecessary concern if a patrol was not immediately contactable. I asked Captain John McPhie, my signals officer, to sort the problem out.

That evening I went flying with one of our pilots, Captain Nigel Thursby, whom I had known since he was a cadet at RMA Sandhurst. He was intent on showing me what could be achieved using the latest image intensification vision aids which effectively allowed the pilot to see, fly and land, in total darkness. The gadget was most impressive, and very daunting to a terrorist I thought. As the weeks went by we made more and more use of the development, especially when deploying or recovering covert patrols.

Despite an excellent night's sleep which restored most of my sleep bank the last day of April started badly for me. We had spent much of the previous week restricting our use of RAF helicopters because there were supposedly too few 'flying hours' available. This had constrained our patrol programme and many patrols had walked where in more normal circumstances they might have flown. We were not best pleased, therefore, to be telephoned at 08.30 that morning and told that we could have 30 hours of flying on that day, simply because it was the last day of the month. This was the classic case of poor management by the RAF staff at HQNI, and I was very annoyed that they could be so inefficient. However, the nonsense served a purpose, and a better control system was devised thereafter.

Later in the morning I went to Lurgan by car for the Brigadier's weekly O Group. Nothing much came of it except a request to dust off our plans to reinforce the Maze prison should we be called to do so. I remember thinking that to extract the battalion for such a task would be both time consuming and unreasonable.

Captain John Williams, one of my two Quartermasters, brought me some interesting news in the late afternoon. In Newry he had come across a civilian whom he recognised as an ex-Parachute Regiment Sergeant. The man had complained that Support Company patrols in Newry were being somewhat beastly to the local population. I was not pleased to hear this but it did confirm what I had suspected. Support Company was attracting quite a lot of adverse publicity in the town and in my experience there was unlikely to be smoke without fire. However, the company always denied the allegations and the locals always exaggerated so it was difficult to know what to believe in the absence of an unbiased third party witness. Now I had one, and I grasped the opportunity without delay. After supper I talked to all the Support Company officers and sergeants and left them in no doubt at all that I would not tolerate any sort of mindless and counter-productive bully boy patrolling.

The day and the month ended pleasantly at the home of the commodore of the Rostrevor Yacht Club, a smart modern home facing south on the shore of Carlingford Lough. My RM detachment often used the Yacht Club slipway for discharging and picking up patrols and he was anxious (and very reasonably so) to ensure that the Marines did not drive their dories too fast amongst the moored yachts and keen also to get a little rental for the use of the slipway. I promised to try; he was helping us and I saw no reason why the Club should not get a little money in return, and I hoped his investment of a couple of beers and some sandwiches would pay off.

# CHAPTER SIX

# Life in the Bases

Our tour in the country had now established itself into a discernible pattern. As most functions were being maintained on a 24 hours a day basis throughout the seven day week everyone was into a sort of routine whilst at the same time being ready, and indeed expecting, to be called upon at very short notice to tackle something unforeseen.

The overall pattern of activity at each company base and battalion HQ was approximately the same. A central core was the continuously manned Army Operations Room and the almost continuously manned RUC Room which were supported by radio operators, clerks and intelligence collators. These Operations Rooms were able to respond to any immediate requests and emergencies, handle the routine, and produce the instructions which were necessary from time to time for special operations. In a nutshell they kept the battalion and RUC day to day activities running harmoniously together yet responsive to the calls of the general public and the actions of the terrorists. They were usually busier and more fully staffed between about 07.00 and 22.00 than at night and as most were situated in windowless rooms, those whose duties required them to spend most of their waking hours there could easily exhaust a complete tour in the dark (and this was especially true at Bessbrook), unless they made a conscious effort to get out on patrol or a visit during their off duty hours.

Guarding every base was a ring of sentry posts or 'sangars'. These were elevated posts constructed of breeze block and steel manned by soldiers working two hours on, four hours off for a day or more. Everyone took their turn for it was a thankless and tedious job. Sentries rarely saw anything suspicious or fired their rifles, but they had to be prepared at all times to make that

**Above** *The operations room at Bessbrook Mill.*

**Below** *Newry Base front entrance. A typical 'sangar' is seen behind the electricity pole draped in camouflage netting and behind anti-rocket wire.*

life or death split second decision. As a deterrent they were vital, for no sensible terrorist who cared for his life (and all did) would produce a bomb or weapon under the nose of a sentry, each of whom was connected by intercom to the Operations Room so if he did see anything remotely suspicious the QRF could be turned out instantly to investigate. Naturally to fall asleep whilst on sentry was regarded as a most heinous crime because an inalert sentry immediately imperilled the lives of his comrades who were relying on his vigilance. It attracted an automatic punishment of jail or field punishment for at least 28 days and, of course, a loss of all pay for the same period. (More recently, sentries have been replaced to some extent by remote-controlled CCTV cameras with a monitor in the Operations Room but that development was in an embryonic state in 1976.)

To ensure that terrorists could not operate at will outside the vision of the sentries local patrols were necessary, particularly within a 500 metre radius to deter a terrorist mortar attack (PIRA have not yet devised a mortar capable of much greater range). These patrols were normally found from the guard platoon whose tasks were also to provide the sentries, the QRF and some of the Operations Room staff. Patrolling outside the base was always a thankless and unpopular chore. It was quite impossible to put out so many patrols as to render terrorist activity very unlikely; consequently terrorists or their associates could watch patrols return to base knowing full well that although another would be out within the next hour or so it would not be around immediately. This gave them ample time to set up an ambush without the burden of having to lie in wait for too long. Of course, patrols were instructed to use different routes but in a small village it was not feasible for patrols to avoid certain obvious choke points particularly very close to the base entrances. So the soldiers felt, and rightly, that every time they went on a local patrol they were being set up as potential targets, they were consequently both keyed up and cautious and therefore easily provoked.

One of the tasks for sentries and local patrols was to feed car numbers into the computer. This was a simple process whereby the sentry or soldier on patrol radioed the vehicle number to his base, the number was typed in on a computer terminal and

*Typical close protection patrols: Forkill (above) and (below) protecting a VCP (in middle distance).*

an instantaneous answer would be given as to whether the vehicle was of interest or not. This was an excellent idea making valuable use of modern technology and we made considerable use of it with occasionally good results. But it could not then cope with British mainland or Southern Irish number plates and the terrorists were not slow to exploit this huge gap in the original software.

The whole equation of numbers available for patrolling was an interesting one. Each Rifle Company was responsible for a TAOR of at least 36 square miles and it consisted of three platoons each of about 24-26 men, plus its command and administrative elements. These three platoons had between them to conduct all the local protective patrols and the more distant patrols within the TAOR, provide the sangar sentries, the QRF, the men to clean the base, and help in the kitchen. The general routine, therefore, was for one platoon to be out on distant patrolling whilst a second platoon provided the local patrols, QRF and sentries, leaving the third to rest and provide the fatigue men. Superimposed on this routine was the need from time to time for two or even three platoons to do something together, such as helping to clear an IED or clear a route for a special road convoy. Company routines thus tended to fall into cycles where platoons did the same thing for two or three days at a stretch thus: three days' distant patrolling, three days' local patrolling and guards, three days' fatigues and rest. From this it is easy to see that the platoon on distant patrolling, patrolling the 36 square miles with three patrols each of eight men, was not likely to be covering much of the ground at any given moment.

Everyone had a place in the base where they kept their kit and could sleep; this was their 'bedspace'. Alluding to these and the general conditions, an *Aldershot News* reporter wrote:

> They are living in terrible conditions, in one base area there are nine men with all their equipment for four months squeezed into a room barely 18 feet by ten. Extra rooms have been made from portable buildings and the overall feeling is that if animals were made to live under similar conditions there would be a hue and cry from the rescue organisations.

The same reporter quoted me as saying, 'It is just like being in prison, but being let out to patrol the area.' What the journalist did not say is that most soldiers' accommodation was wall to

*Confined spaces: living accommodation at Crossmaglen (above) and car parking at Crossmaglen (below).*

**Above** *Luxury – garden sheds at Forkill.*

**Below** *Forkill. Corporals Goodrich, Gow, Shearer and Bradley playing Scrabble.*

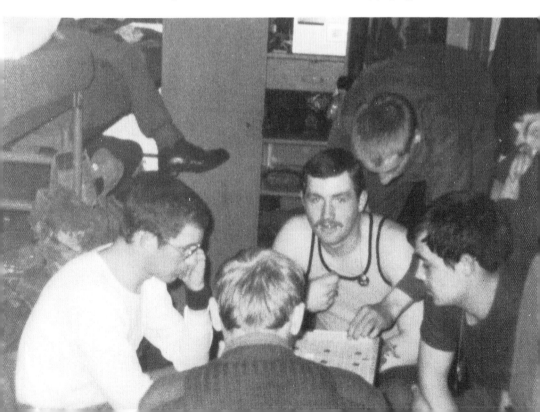

ceiling papered with nudes from a variety of pornographic magazines so that busts, pubic hair and obscene poses literally surrounded them. This 'wallpaper' was not the result of much initiative by my soldiers, but rather the accumulated product of the many previous inhabitants. Few mothers would have condoned such blatant male chauvinism but it was pretty harmless and undeniably brightened up their surroundings.

Unquestionably I had about the best room in the battalion. It was rather dark, cold and bleak but there was space for a bed and desk, and I had that most precious commodity, privacy. Like everyone else I lived 'on top of the shop', in my case some 20 metres down the corridor from my Operations Room. Most of my officers and SNCOs were much worse off and many had to share rooms barely the size of cupboards. For junior NCOs and soldiers the best accommodation was often a converted garden shed with two double bunks on each side and into which four men had to cram their kit which included (when they returned from patrol) wet and smelly sleeping bags, boots, clothing and equipment. The sheer claustrophobic congestion is difficult to imagine. Every available inch of space was taken up with extensions to kitchens, lean-tos, stores, wash rooms, showers, portakabins, lavatories, dining areas, canteens, ammunition, fuel, helicopter landing sites and radio antennae.

Each base had at least one 'Char Wallah' who operated the canteen. Char Wallahs were employed by a Pakistani contractor who had tendered for the privilege of running the canteen service for our tour. The arrangement was that he had to provide the service at pre-arranged prices and on that basis he worked out his possible profit. He could sell a variety of items but largely hot and cold drinks, hot snacks, chocolate and cigarettes, and he was awarded the contract partly on the size of his tender (at that time about £4,000) and partly on patronage – the battalion usually favouring the reliable man it knew rather than an unknown quantity.

In this instance I had taken on Jan Mohommad, the contractor who was serving the previous battalion, 1 RS. I did this because I was impressed by the way in which he had organised matters. For the most part his employees were clean and willing and were familiar with helicopter resupply, for at Forkill and Crossmaglen all the contractors' goodies were moved to the bases by air. He also knew the form in South Armagh for unquestionably profits there were much lower than in Belfast because soldiers spent so little time in the bases, so he had the experience of 1 RS on which to frame his tender. Despite my verbal warning to him he assumed that my soldiers would consume a fair amount of beer despite the official restriction to two pints a day but in the event they consumed so little that his profit was much less than he anticipated. Astute businessman that he was he came to me before the end of the tour pleading for a refund, but I felt obliged to hold him to the original contract. Undeterred and far from destitute he was keen to offer his services two years later when 3 PARA next returned to Ulster.

Just as the friendly launderette is a focal point of social activity in many of our cities so the washing and drying machines in each base were a meeting place. The machines worked around the clock, literally, for although there was also a contract laundry facility it was generally inconvenient to send too much away for a whole week. So washing, ironing and mending became a fundamental part of the routine for everyone in their off duty hours. Mending particularly. The thick blackthorn hedges and barbed wire fences played havoc with our parachute smock (jackets) and trousers and most received huge tears during the course of the tour but only those which were beyond redemption were actually replaced.

The poor quality of the accommodation was more than compensated for by the excellent comradeship and stagger- ingly good food. One aspect of the British Army which has been improved beyond all recognition in the last twenty years is the training and quality of the cooks. The conditions in which they worked were pretty awful yet in a company base the three cooks provided three hot meals a day for a moving population of between 20 and 120, often at very irregular times. That they managed it at all was astonishing as most kitchens were tiny and certainly not constructed with an eye to efficiency, many were not much more than corridors, but to manage to provide both choice and excellent quality was truly miraculous. The most popular men in each company were therefore the cooks (although few soldiers would have admitted it and most spent their time teasing them in a lighthearted and harmless way).

**Above** *Helicopter re-supply.*

**Below** *The cookhouse at Bessbrook Mill.*

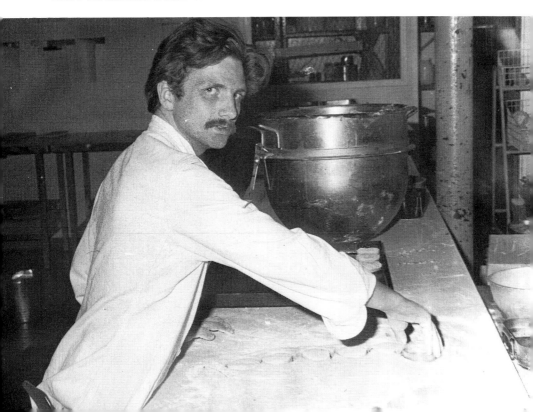

A short head behind in the popularity stakes was often the Char Wallah for by working at least an eighteen-hour day he could earn the respect and indeed affection of the soldiers. As with the cooks, such affection showed itself in funny ways, because the Char Wallah was more often than not cheerfully insulted to his face. Indeed throughout every base there was always a thread of high but crude good humour. The British soldier is at his best in adversity and rarely wasted his time moaning about conditions. The worse the conditions are, the more we British laugh, so there was always plenty of laughter around.

What was totally absent was peace and quiet. Added to the racket of people, radios, TV, generators, was the additional clatter of helicopters arriving and departing, the metallic clang as the heavy corrugated iron gates were opened and shut to allow through a patrol but most disturbing of all, the heavy thump, thump of the pipe range. The latter was simply a 20-metre concrete tube about two feet in diameter with a target at one end. To keep check of his rifle's accuracy each soldier was obliged to fire it about once a week and obviously the echo of a high velocity weapon being discharged within a concrete tube was irritating to say the least. Probably the only time that a soldier was left with his own thoughts was when he was on sentry but there was absolutely nowhere he could sit and relax alone. So he was either working or in bed (asleep, reading, listening to music or thinking warm thoughts about the wallpaper), eating, doing his domestic chores, or in the canteen where there was a TV and he could play simple time-passing games with his mates (draughts, scrabble, monopoly, darts, cards and the like). More often than not he was either on duty or asleep.

The telephone was the best link to wives and girlfriends but it was always a bone of contention that telephone calls to GB were very expensive (even at the cheaper rates allowed) and they were difficult to make or receive. There were few telephones so a booking system was organised for those that existed. For the less fortunate soldiers whose loved ones did not have a telephone at home, making contact was exceedingly tricky. If the wife or girlfriend called Ulster it was expensive and the chance of finding their man in was remote. If the call went the

*Taking exercise at Forkill.*

other way it probably had to be to a pre-arranged number (often a road side telephone kiosk) frequently very late at night so contact with loved ones was consequently tenuous in the extreme. The lucky ones were those who worked in Operations Rooms and offices who could often sneak a call to GB by using the military phone unofficially, and those who had a telephone at home. For myself I was able to telephone Paddy daily; this was a godsend.

Trying to keep fit was also very difficult. When on patrol, caution, and therefore slow movement was the order of the day and although this was tiring it did not really make anyone fit. To get fit means working up a sweat and there really are only two methods; exercises and running. The latter was virtually impossible although many tried running round and round minute areas, 100 laps of the Bessbrook heli-pad (the largest area in the battalion) only totalled five miles, but running outside the bases was absolutely out of the question – it was far too dangerous. Luckily each base had a multi-gym, another shed with inside a contraption of stainless steel, springs and weights which enabled a number of men to exercise simultaneously and develop most muscles in their bodies. They were very popular and in heavy demand, even in the middle of the night. Just how unfit many of us were we were to discover later in the tour, but we did try to do something from time to time, although I must confess that I was more idle than most.

# CHAPTER SEVEN

# Border Incursions

## *1st-14th May 1976*

On 1st May 1976 a new Chief Constable, Kenneth Newman (later Sir Kenneth Newman, Chief Commissioner of the Metropolitan Police) was appointed to the RUC. A Scotland Yard policeman he had spent three years as deputy to Sir James Flanagan, the retiring Chief and now headed the 5,000 strong force. A small, dapper, highly intelligent and articulate man Newman had firm ideas on police primacy and how the RUC should be organised and develop. He looked forward to the day when the Army could pull out leaving the RUC in control, but he was a realist and knew it would not happen quickly. He believed in sensitive policing using all the technical developments which became available, and intended that the RUC would gradually change from a reactive force to one with a more positive role of prevention. Essentially though he was a pragmatist and saw the need for the force to be equipped with high velocity rifles and armoured landrovers if they were to have any chance against armed criminals and terrorists. Kenneth Newman's new role was described by the *Sunday Times* as 'The man in the hottest police seat in Europe'. I do not think that anyone would have argued with that.

For 3 PARA, May was to become a month of border incursions but it started innocuously enough. Andrew returned from burying his father so my battalion HQ team was back to full strength. However, I was having great problems on the intelligence side. My IO seemed to be asking companies for far too much daily paperwork, so that at company level working time was being spent on the wrong activities. I devoted some time to trying to re-direct the company intelligence staffs who had collected at battalion HQ for their weekly get together.

Certainly there was an acute lack of confidence between the Support Company IO in Newry (where there was some intelligence) and the battalion IO, and I knew that this was a problem which would not disappear overnight. The former had real flair for intelligence work but preferred to work intuitively, whereas the latter lacking the instinct thought more in terms of reports and other written detail. The clash was therefore fundamental.

It was a Saturday, and as quite frequently happened at the weekends, a company of UDR soldiers from Belfast had been sent to me for use over the two days. This company passed by the rather grand title of Province Reserve UDR (PRUDR) but what it meant was a bunch of largely part-time and barely trained soldiers normally from the City of Belfast transported to the countryside for a weekend. The difficulty was making use of their talents (they were quite good at searching buildings, stone walls, hedgerows and the like for weapons or explosives) whilst not putting them at risk nor placing them where they could come into much contact with the public. On this occasion we had asked them to search an unpopulated area between Camlough and Silverbridge and I took the opportunity to fly out to visit them. It was a rotten day, wet and windy, yet they seemed very content but hopelessly at sea in that unfamiliar rural environment and I did not rate their chances very high if they were attacked by terrorists. Most importantly, however, they felt that they were deep in 'bandit country' so I knew that on this occasion at least I would not be pilloried on Monday for failing to provide a sufficient challenge for them.

There were two shooting incidents during the day at fairly predictable spots; Monog, south of Crossmaglen and Cullyhanna. Both were targeted at A Company patrols and one was mounted from just outside the post office in Cullyhanna – a place I knew well from my last tour because the postmaster, who had been civil to us, was bombed out of his livelihood for his good manners. In both cases the patrols returned fire and we were pleased to discover two days later that one Colm Murphy had been hit in the knee at the first incident and then arrested by the Garda when he reported to hospital in the Republic.

That evening I went to a cocktail party at Brigade HQ followed by supper at the Brigadier's house. I recorded in my diary that it appeared that he would be replaced in command before the end of our tour 'which is a great pity for David Anderson is a very sensible, down to earth soldier who will support one in most eventualities'. Clearly and despite getting my knuckles wrapped more than once I was very content with my immediate superior.

Sunday was another social day. At lunchtime I attended a party given by 1 Green Howards at Portadown. It was really surprising that there were any parties at all and even more that I found time and felt the need to attend them. The fact is that they were really a form of 'business entertainment' and in this case it was 1 Green Howards' way of thanking all those with whom they had had dealings during their short Spearhead tour.

On my return journey I called in at Newtownhamilton to see Ian and then on my way to Bessbrook stopped to examine an abandoned Mini near Camlough which was currently under investigation as a possible ambush (I was in civilian clothes so I considered I was safe). I recorded in my diary that the patch of earth which the Reconnaissance Intelligence Centre (RIC) aerial photographs of the site had indicated as suspicious (possibly concealing buried explosive) was very old and I personally doubt whether there is much in this'. This proved correct, for the following day the Mini was driven away by its owner, a most satisfactory outcome.

In the early evening I went to Crossmaglen to join a town patrol led by Julian James. He was a small, bright and sparky young officer who had recently joined the battalion from university and I was delighted with the way in which he handled the patrol and by the alertness and professionalism of his soldiers. It was my first time on town patrol in Crossmaglen since 1973 and I was interested in the changes which had taken place. Generally it was more run down and less friendly (if that was possible) than it had been then and even their ebullient local publican and spokesman, Paddy Short, seemed a bit subdued. The tension and length of the campaign was clearly having an effect. After the patrol I remained in Crossmaglen for a while talking through our tactics with Colin until about 23.30 when I flew back to Bessbrook.

Monday started unpleasantly for I had decided to get a firm

grip of the intelligence section which I was most unhappy with. The final straw had occurred over the weekend when their photographer got drunk and their Corporal with two others used their car to attend a dance at the army HQ at Lisburn and successfully wrote it off on the way back. Half the trouble lay with the Army's Northern Ireland tradition that intelligence staffs worked in plain clothes, were allowed to grow their hair long and had civilian cars available for their use. In no time at all they seemed to forget that they were soldiers and subject to military discipline. From that Monday I ordered them to work in uniform and cut their hair. I took away the car and gave out a few rockets I hoped they would remember. The Corporal was fined £90 for crashing the car and several other men were removed although I was most reluctant to do too much because I was jeopardising the priceless requirement of continuity in intelligence work. However, I hoped that this purge would have a good enough effect, although I was not confident that it would provide a complete recipe.

After a short visit to Forkill to talk to Malcolm I was visited at Bessbrook by Seamus Mallon, ex Convention member, member of the Social Democratic and Labour Party (SDLP) part-time teacher, part-time protester. He came at my invitation and we had a fairly pleasant chat. I recorded that:

> I think we are agreed on basics and he ventured that there was an obvious disenchantment between the PIRA and the people who were beginning to see them in their true light as Mafia type bully boys and thugs. He also suggested that although they professed Republicanism the people of South Armagh and Crossmaglen in particular stood only to lose if they became part of the Republic.

I told him that our policy was to arrest or kill terrorists and be kind and pleasant to everyone else, so the law abiding public need have no worries about us.

In the evening, after telephoning Paddy, who had taken some wives and families to Chessington Zoo, I went down to Newry to join a Support Company mobile patrol through all the least attractive estates. It was all very quiet. Joe Baker had been asked by SB to arrange for the arrest of a number of

people the following morning and was busy planning the operation. At 01.30 an 80 lb bomb exploded in one of Newry's main
streets; the device had been behind a wall and was detonated by
command wire. It was clearly intended for an Army patrol, so
why it was fired when no patrol was around was a complete
mystery. Certainly it could have killed a few soldiers as it threw
the wall right across the road – yet again we had been fortunate.

Tuesday, 4th May, was the usual day of meetings. At my O
Group I was able to congratulate A Company on actually hitting
a terrorist and thank the two companies from the Green Howards who were due to leave the following day. It was therefore
most inopportune that we learnt at 08.30 on the Wednesday that
nine men, of whom two were re-captured very quickly, had
tunnelled out of the Maze Prison some three hours earlier. The
plan to close all routes leading to the Republic was instantly
activated, but it was far too late. For us it was very bad news, not
solely because it takes months of effort to get men behind bars.
The realisation that terrorists are being allowed to escape faster
than we could arrest them was most disheartening, but more
important for me, we had to provide a string of VCPs on a day
when we were losing the two Green Howard companies and
handing over Newtownhamilton to 1 QLR. However, I decided
to press on regardless and as I flew round to check that everything was running smoothly, I was impressed by the phlegmatic
way in which everyone was getting on with the job despite the
additional burden. The 4th Royal Tank Regiment (4 RTR) who
were responsible at the time for guarding the Maze were not the
most popular regiment in Ulster that day. They had a rotten and
unenviable job but that was no excuse for not doing it well.

After lunch I was visited by the head of MI5 and a gaggle of
Security Service men. I talked to them for a very short time and
then spent well over an hour answering questions. I tried to
impress on them the need to control explosive detonators in the
Republic and in the UK and at the end of the discussion I took
Sir 'M' round the border in my Gazelle. His afternoon clearly
pleased him, for in his thank you letter he was kind enough to
write, 'Your presentation of the IRA threat from across the
border was the best I have ever heard, the most detailed, and
certainly the most convincing.'

My quiet evening was enlivened by Paddy who seemed thrilled

# PATRICK ST, NEWRY 4 MAY

<u>80 lbs</u> of Explosives

behind the garden wall

<u>Detonated</u> by electric wire

from the other side of the playground

<u>Exploded</u> at 1.15 am

<u>Six</u> people treated for shock and bruises

## But

# NO ARMY OR RUC PATROL WAS IN THE VICINITY

by the attendance at a wives' party she had held that evening. It was clear that she and Captain Mick Edney (the families officer) were getting on well together, with Mick doing most of the work – just as it should be. I was in bed by 24.00 which was fortunate, for at 03.00 on Thursday 6 May I was woken with the glad tidings that three SAS cars had crossed the border into the Republic and the eight soldiers arrested.

The SAS squadron commander was not sure what had happened and could only guess, but it appeared that when one of his cars on a reconnaissance task which took them very close to the border became overdue at about midnight, a pair of cars were sent from Bessbrook at 01.30 to look for it. He assumed that all three cars had made the same map-reading error and finished up just across the border at an Irish checkpoint where they were arrested. I immediately contacted our RUC liaison officer at Bessbrook, whose main job was to maintain sweet contacts with his opposite numbers in the Garda to try and obtain their quick release but he got no joy, so I left Andrew Dudzinski to stay up to monitor the situation whilst I returned to bed.

I was not at all worried about the incident, soldiers frequently crossed the border in error and I had known RAF helicopters deposit whole platoons up to a mile inside the Republic without any fuss being made. The normal drill was that the Irish lodged a token protest to our Embassy in Dublin and we reported the transgression formally up the military net so that when the request came to our Defence Adviser in Dublin for an explanation, one was readily to hand. The Irish Army had also on occasion crossed into the North so it never occurred to me that in this instance the Irish would take a different line. (Indeed on 14th May the *Irish News* gave the following figures for unauthorised crossings: 47 in 1973, 121 in 1974, 68 in 1975).

I got up late (07.50) and was just shaving and listening to Radio Ulster in my room when Captain Richard Hoyle (my adjutant) came in to tell me that the SAS OC and I were to be in CLF's office in Lisburn at 08.30. I was surprised that the SAS men had not been released but I dressed quickly and just managed a quick coffee before flying to Lisburn 35 miles away. Thanks to the helicopter we arrived just in time, but a little breathless. CLF and Brigadier David were already waiting and we were asked for an explanation.

The squadron commander gave this and there was a visible and almost audible sigh of relief that we had not been indulging in cross-border patrolling which, of course, was absolutely forbidden. From their point of view a serious cross-border incident was the last thing they needed following as it did the disaster of the Maze breakout the previous day. They did not know it at the time, but the SAS incident would totally eclipse the Maze story. Indeed I was quite surprised that when Brigadier David visited me at Bessbrook later in the morning he was pretty cheerful, which said a lot for him because although neither incident could in any way be attributed directly to him he was ultimately the person who carried the responsibility.

The nausea (for that is what it became) of the SAS men really hit the headlines on the BBC and Ulster TV programmes that evening. Although we were not ourselves certain of the true story, and would not be until we had talked to our eight men, we found the speculative journalism, each reporter trying to outdo the next in his fanciful ideas of 'what the SAS were really doing', very irritating. Eventually, quite late in the day the Republic decided to charge the men with possessing weapons and ammunition with intent to endanger life and having no Southern Irish firearms certificate and they were released on £5,000 bail each and flown out by RAF Puma to Bessbrook, and then quickly on to HQNI at Lisburn for questioning by the RMP SIB. Her Majesty's Government stood surety.

Apart from all this, which I was not directly involved in because it was being dealt with at HQNI/MOD level, that Thursday was just another day. I spent the afternoon in Jonesborough with Malcolm talking to the villagers and others at the weekly open air market. I was surprised how willing they were to indulge in a proper conversation despite being very firm Republicans. Their main concern was whether the market was a help or a nuisance. Most of them thought that it just produced a mass of litter, whereas the garage owner was very keen – no doubt he profited greatly from the event. Then I flew to Crossmaglen, which was a lot tidier than of late, and that evening down to Newry. Joe was naturally uneasy about my attitude to the flood of complaints, which were appearing in the Press and local propaganda broadsheets, about Support Company's attitude to the local people. Our chat cleared the air, but I was adamant that there is rarely smoke without fire.

The following day, 7th May, the news was all SAS and the eight soldiers were still being questioned at Lisburn at 08.30. Also in the news that morning was the sad story that three officers from 1 Green Howards had been killed in a car crash just outside their camp in Chester on the previous day – the day they returned from their Spearhead tour in Ulster.

After attending the Brigade O Group I was due for a visit from the GOC at lunchtime. Whilst waiting for him to arrive I learnt that at 11.30 there had been another border crossing. This time the story seemed far less believable as it had occurred on the main Dublin road, in daylight when three landrovers (two of mine and one RUC with an officer, nine soldiers and two RUC officers) crossed into the Republic. In a way it could not have happened at a worse time, but it did show very graphically how easy it was and how often mistakes were made. Indeed some journalists were to accuse us of crossing deliberately. The GOC, bless him, was very calm and we went ahead with his visit to everyone at Bessbrook and each company base. He left in good humour promising me a bottle of champagne if we removed a terrorist from the scene.

At 21.30 that evening there occurred a brilliant example of the luck of the Irish. A bomb went off outside Tully's Bar in Belleek. The UVF clearly suspected that it was a PIRA meeting place and the bomb was clearly a UVF effort. The heavy outside steel door against which the bomb had been planted, was blown straight down a passage and across the bar, a distance of 40 yards. The pub was not crowded, but nor was it empty, yet not a soul was even scratched. Tully himself was drinking on the other side of the border and when he returned he demanded to know why we were not giving him protection. I had gone out to the incident as it was an excellent opportunity to have a look around the bar, but in the end it was with difficulty that I avoided an unpleasant slanging match with Tully. I was back in Bessbrook by 00.30.

Brigadier David arrived at 09.00 for a chat and to be present when the Secretary of State, Merlyn Rees, who was due to visit at 09.50 arrived. The latter eventually turned up at 10.30, his car having broken down. He seemed very relaxed, nevertheless, and I was delighted that he was both robust and supportive over our border incidents. Indeed he was furious about the Dublin Government's attitude and affirmed that the Prime Minister was also. I took him around the Mill and then to Crossmaglen, persuading him en route that cross-border co-operation had not improved a fraction over the past three years despite reports from his own office suggesting the opposite. On the late night radio news he was reported as condemning the Irish Government for mishandling the whole affair and suggesting it would be a tragedy if the men were ever brought to trial.

Earlier in the evening I had had to warn Roger Miller to be much more careful about whom he sent out at night. I had discovered that on the previous night a young lance-corporal who did not know the area, had been foolishly sent out alone to recover a broken down covert car from a spot very close to the border. This broke all the rules (he was too inexperienced, travelling alone and going very close to the border) but luckily he made it there and back without incident. Had he made a mistake and crossed the border or worse, been involved in an ambush, I suspected that there would have been a new CO in 3 PARA, and rightly so. This highlighted the dilemma everyone had. Manpower was tight and we were working at full stretch, so when something happened which demanded a quick response it was frequently not possible to obey all the rules, to do so could easily put someone's life at risk. But to flout them also put lives at risk.

Saturday night and early Sunday were quite busy. A bomb left outside the Newry RUC station was defused by my ATO; the RUC in Rostrevor had a skirmish with some youths; and a B Company covert search for a bomb with the help of an intelligence officer from Brigade HQ proved successful when they located 900 lbs of home-made explosive packed in milkchurns.

The Sunday newspapers (9th May) were full of the SAS business and it is probably appropriate here to discuss what had happened in that incident and the incident the following day. The tale was really very straightforward: two SAS men had been tasked with a reconnaissance of a possible OP. Their plan was to conduct this on foot and in uniform, but as was normal in these instances they were to be taken to the area and recovered by a civilian car manned by two armed soldiers in plain clothes. Before leaving Bessbrook they lodged their intended route and return time with their squadron operations room. The intention was that the civilian car would return to Bessbrook after dropping off the reconnaissance party and await a call from them on the radio before proceeding to the pick up. In the event, some time after midnight the Duty Operations Officer realised the car had not returned to Bessbrook. He let some time elapse and then alerted four more soldiers whom he sent out in two civilian cars to pick up the reconnaissance party and to look for the first car.

As we learnt subsequently, the first car had in fact accidentally driven over the border at Cornamucklagh (H2) at approximately 22.50 where the Garda, supported by the Irish Army, were manning a check point; this was only a very short time after dropping off their passengers. Why at that time the Garda had not contacted us, or anyone in Ulster, remains a complete mystery, for had they done so there would have been no requirement to send the search party.

Before sending out the second party the Duty Officer briefed them on the route and possible difficulties. In the minds of the rescue party anything could have occurred from a vehicle accident to an ambush. A simple breakdown was unlikely for the first car had a radio, and even if that had not been working they could have been anticipated to make contact, so they expected the worst. As we now know, the second party picked up the reconnaissance party and then proceeded along the route the first car should have taken back to Bessbrook when they succeeded in making the same map reading error. The media, not unreasonably, simply could not believe that two patrols from the most highly trained military force in the world could commit 'map-reading errors'. But the fact is that they did and having later examined the route myself, it is easy enough to see how the mistakes occurred.

All three cars were travelling a narrow border road in what we regarded as PIRA territory in the dark. The soldiers would have been very alert; in the first car only the passenger could be ready to use his weapon should they get ambushed, and he was also the map reader. Nothing would have drawn attention to the car more effectively than being seen to be map-reading, so the map was kept out of sight and used as infrequently as possible. Looking at the map, the indication was that having reached Clontygora (Edenfore) crossroads the road going east led up to and then along the border until it came to a 'T' junction about 1½ miles away. At the 'T' junction their route was to turn north (left) past Flagstaff Hill.

Here I should draw attention to the map. Two scales of map cover were in use in South Armagh. There was an excellent series of maps at 1:20,000 scale which showed every house and hedgerow and these were used principally by the companies. They were particularly useful on foot patrol and were vital for enabling patrols to know exactly where the border ran. Because of their large scale, seven full map sheets (each 3 feet × 2 feet) were needed to provide coverage of the battalion area, so except when involved in a short term foot patrol those of us based at Bessbrook and travelling throughout the battalion area by car or helicopter used a one inch to one mile scale map only two feet square which covered the whole area.

The one-inch map we thought was just the less detailed version of the two maps, but it transpired that it was drawn quite differently to the 1:20,000 map, and there was a most significant discrepancy between them in the area of Cornamucklagh border crossings. The one inch map, as can be seen, shows a definite 'T' junction some 200-300 metres west of the border whereas the 1:20,000 shows that the 'T' junction does not exist, and that the road from Edenfore curves gently across the stream and into the Republic. So for these SAS patrols, using the smaller scale map at night and expecting a 'T' junction, it was very, very easy indeed to drive straight into the Republic.

Why Dublin reacted in the way it did, charging the men and subsequently bringing them to trial, will probably remain a mystery. However, Christopher Walker, in an article in *The Times* on 19th May 1976 must have been very close to the mark when he wrote:

'The main difficulty with Anglo-Irish relations', a senior British official explained, 'is that if either of us is scratched

*Map discrepancies. Very different road junctions are contained within the circles on the two maps of different scales: the 1:63,360 (one inch to one mile) scale which we all carried (above) and the 1:20,000 scale showing much more detail (below).*

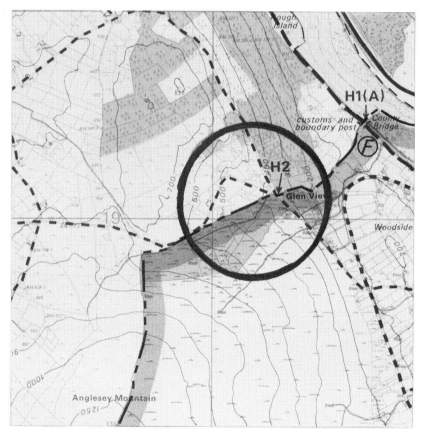

just below the surface there is an awful lot of history lurking to affect and inflame attitudes'. His point was proved last week with the decision to prosecute eight members of the SAS after their arrest at Flagstaff Hill [sic], about 550 yards south of the border. Had the eight been ordinary, uniformed squaddies, there is little doubt that, in spite of the repeated claims about the independence of the Irish Judiciary they would have been returned to the North with nothing but red faces and bruised egos.

However, the SAS has, in the last few years of the Ulster crisis, acquired a reputation in the South similar to that of the hated Black and Tans in the early twenties. Among Irishmen of all political shades, the folk tales of their undercover activities and alleged mastery of 'dirty tricks' are firmly believed, and provide the background to the trial soon to take place in Dublin.

The *Newry Reporter* on 20th May linked the SAS incident with the incident the following day when the three landrovers crossed into the Republic:

The claim, by the British Army, that their crack regiment cannot read maps is somewhat incredible and was not helped by the clumsy attempt to repeat the 'mistake' the next day with a joint British Army-RUC patrol. This patrol, which included RUC men, with an intimate knowledge of the area, is supposed to have passed the unmistakable remains of the largest customs post in the country, on the main Belfast-Dublin road past a number of signs welcoming them to the South of Ireland and driven to the Southern Customs post without realising where they were. To be asked to believe this is stretching our faith in the stupidity of the British Army and RUC too far.

Those incidents would be laughable if it was not for the very sinister role played by the SAS. Already they have acknowledged responsibility for one death in this area, i.e. the brutal murder of Peter Cleary.

What had happened in the second border incursion was also pretty straightforward. Southern Ireland exports commercial explosive for quarrying to Ulster and from time to time a joint RUC and Army escort meets the vehicles coming up from the Republic at the border and accompanies them to their destination. The escort on 7th May was the first such task to occur during our tour. The orders for the convoy had been issued by Brigade HQ some years previously and were passed over to us by 1 RS. Two Army Landrovers in the charge of an officer had to meet up with and escort an RUC landrover. The 3 PARA officer selected and briefed was Lieutenant Tim Hollis and at the appointed time the three landrovers met up in Newry and proceeded south, with the RUC leading towards the selected meeting place on the main road to Dublin. Lieutenant Hollis had not been along that road previously but not unnaturally he assumed that the RUC had, and knew what they were doing. Clearly Tim was mistaken and they did not, for in no time at all the three vehicles were in the Republic. Luckily, on this occasion there was no question of arrest, but Tim had to give a detailed account to the RMP SIB. This report was duly studied by CLF and the brigade commander. Far from this being a contrived incident as suggested in the press it became quite a nausea. Brigadier David wrote to me dated 12th May:

As we discussed, the briefing and conduct of the operation was bad, with no liaison between the RUC and the officer concerned. It is quite inexcusable that the officer did not even read his map and I just do not understand why he was unaware of the location and condition of the Kileen Customs Post.

You must be in no doubt that CLF and I are most displeased over the whole incident and you are to take all the necessary steps urgently to ensure that similar incidents, or indeed any cross-border incursions do not occur again.

Please draw the attention of those concerned to my remarks.

I was not able to reply immediately but I did so on 16th May:

Thank you for your letter of 12 May 1976. Although I do not for one minute condone the action of Lt Hollis in not reading his map I do not think that it is entirely fair to make him scapegoat for an unfortunate incident. Had I thought that the incident was caused solely by his idleness I would have dealt with him immediately and I have made it quite clear to him that he is far from blameless.

The orders at the time of the incident, and as handed to 3 PARA by 1 RS did not include:

a. The grid reference (GR) of the Kileen Customs Post.
b. A description or photograph of the Kileen Post.
c. A clear statement about responsibility for the conduct of the convoy.

In this I blame myself entirely and quite clearly I should not have accepted the thoroughly vague and ambiguous orders which had been used in the past, without question. The Brigade Major has amended the orders and a GR of the Kileen Post is now included. We have produced a folder of photographs so that the convoy can be in no doubt as to the destination. However there is still no clear statement about responsibility and as we read the instructions the escort commander is an escort to the RUC who are in charge. It is not crystal clear however and I think that it would be helpful if the position was clarified.

I am satisfied that the briefing arrangements now, and indeed before the incident, are satisfactory. At fault previously was the content of the briefing which has now been rectified (with the exception of the definition of responsibility).

I trust that both the CLF and yourself will have no further reason to question our efficiency.

I hoped that that would be the end of border incursions, although my experience in 1973 told me that it was most unlikely to be.

But in the intervening period between 7th May and this exchange of letters the Army swung into automatic over-reaction about the border. On Monday, 10th May, Brigadier David's deputy, Colonel Ian Meynell, came down to Bessbrook to suggest marking all the border crossings. This had been done several years ago and the paint had either by 1976 worn thin, or had been removed by the locals. To undertake such a marking programme would have involved full scale clearance operations at each crossing – for once the PIRA realised what we were up to it would have been child's play for them to ambush (by laying landmines) one or more sites. My answer to Ian was that the Southern Irish, if they felt so strongly, should do the marking on their side for they were not PIRA targets and could carry out the same programme quickly and without difficulty (this was the real irritant that on our side of the border we had to move very carefully whereas the Garda and Irish Army could go wherever they wished in the Republic without risk).

In August 40 Commando RM was due to take over from 3 PARA and Lieutenant-Colonel Julian Thompson (the CO) arrived with two of his officers for their first look at South Armagh. They had arrived on a very quiet day; for the first time in the tour two of my companies had nothing at all to report. After supper Julian (who was later to become well known as the commander of 3 Commando Brigade which formed the bulk of the ground force which re-took the Falkland Islands) and I had a very useful chat until about 23.30.

The following day, 11th May, we escorted a huge convoy of vehicles packed with building materials and tarmacadam to Forkill where we were going to rebuild the perimeter fence so that helicopters could land inside (instead of just outside), to remove and replace some of the huts and generally tidy up the whole of the outside area. Escorting such a convoy meant that the route from Newry to Forkill had to be checked in advance for landmines and then guarded. As the distance was about nine miles it used up quite a bit of manpower.

In addition to the usual Tuesday meetings there was also a Local Security Committee meeting which on this occasion was held in Newry Town Hall at 16.00. This turned out to be a real slanging match with almost everyone criticising Support Company in Newry for being 'rude, brutal, oppressive etc'. The only person able to cite a specific case was Jim Murphy who had two quite well documented examples which I promised to enquire into. The meeting developed into a straightforward match between myself and the Republican councillors with everyone else (military, RUC and Unionist councillors) watching. Evidently, they felt very strongly and there must

*Hollis and his patrol.*

have been, as I had discussed with Joe Baker on several occasions, substance in the allegations. Thankfully I extracted myself in time to catch a flight from Aldergrove to Heathrow at 19.00 for I had to attend a regimental postings conference in Aldershot on the three following days. I arrived home at 22.20 in record time to find Hill House as immaculate and welcoming as always, and Paddy looking quite stunning and very sun-tanned.

I managed to get back to Bessbrook by 18.10 on the Friday, 14th May, just ten minutes late for a briefing on Operation Pike, an operation which we had been planning for two weeks. Essentially it was to be a 'coat-trailing' operation to the south and east of Crossmaglen in which a number of covert OPs would cover the movements of an overt patrol. The hope was that the patrol would attract the attention of PIRA who would try to ambush it. Its route was sufficiently far into the North to force anyone wishing to attack it to come into the North and our OPs were very close to the border, able to cut off any escape route. As it happened the weather that evening was foul so I postponed the start of the operation for 24 hours.

# CHAPTER EIGHT

# More Border Madness

## *15th-31st May 1976*

On Saturday 15th May our second month started well enough. The building convoy was escorted back from Forkill where the change in the general orderliness of the base was nothing short of dramatic. It incidentally meant that when I visited I could park my helicopter inside the base instead of it having to fly back to Bessbrook which had previously wasted precious flying hours and fuel.

In the morning a routine patrol led by Captain Clint Hicks the C Company second-in-command discovered seven beer kegs, each containing 100 lbs of home-made explosive in a shed belonging to Mullen's Garage, astride the border at Flurry-bridge. The garage complex literally straddles the border and on this occasion the Garda were most cooperative, asking for assistance from my patrol to search the part of the garage which was on their side of the border, although perversely they would not arrest the garage owner who was present. This was an excellent find but the RUC (not the local division) were infuriating because they could not or would not produce a scene of crimes officer (SOCO) so the beer kegs were neither finger-printed nor handled correctly. Consequently all we actually achieved was the destruction of 700 lbs of explosive, rather than an arrest or the acquisition of first class evidence leading to arrests. It was frustrating in the extreme.

At 11.20 we were visited for an hour at Bessbrook by the Labour Party Defence Group. It included a most interesting man, Lieutenant-Colonel Dick Crawshaw, a barrister who as a Territorial Army (TA) officer had commanded a TA Parachute Battalion. He was MP for the Toxteth Division of Liverpool and holder of the world non-stop walking record of

255 miles which he established in 1972 at the age of 55. It was an honour to meet such a man.

More and more evidence was piling up to confirm that Support Company patrols were not working as sensitively as they might in Newry. This time my information came from both the UDR and the Military Intelligence Officer (MIO) attached to the RUC at Newry. Yet again I discussed the problem with Joe Baker. Part of the problem was that some of the Support Company NCOs and, I suspected, a number of the officers too thought that I was being wet, and a victim of PIRA's propaganda.

At midnight Edward Gardener came to my room to give me the bad news that Sergeant Hunter of the RUC had been murdered and two reserve constables seriously injured when their car was ambushed at Warrenpoint. I did not go down to Warrenpoint as the incident was already over, but the following day I saw the Chief Superintendent to commiserate with him. He showed me the car, which was a nasty mess and so riddled with bullet holes that it was fortunate that all three men had not been killed.

In the early hours of Sunday Operation Pike started, but the weather was again very miserable and I was not at all sanguine. On wet days the PIRA preferred to stay in or go to the pub so in South Armagh terrorism tended to be confined to the better weather. Certainly nothing happened on this occasion, and the ambush OPs were withdrawn at midnight.

That Sunday was also my birthday, a date which I shared with Joe Baker. I had intended to go down to Newry to have a drink with him and relieve the tension that was growing between us but events conspired against the plan and he never learnt of my good intentions. The reason was that the moving VCP on the Dublin Road became involved in two shooting incidents which although inconclusive took some time to resolve, so that by the time they were, another birthday had passed uncelebrated.

Despite the foul weather, I managed on Monday to get round all the company bases and deal with several military visitors, one of whom was Brigadier David Woodford, the new brigade commander, who needed a full briefing. In the early evening I called in Tim Hollis to tell him formally that we did

# SEVEN BEER KEGS

Filled with 700lbs of explosives
by the Provisional IRA

## WERE FOUND HERE AT
# FLURRYBRIDGE

on 15 May 1976
and made safe by the Army

*Incident at Flurrybridge.*

not think much of his map reading, and then left with a clear conscience to have dinner in Portadown with the two Brigadiers. Tim was later to join the Metropolitan Police so his ideas on the police were clearly not shaken by this incident.

The following day we escorted another large construction convoy, this time to Crossmaglen. There and back in the day. One result was that a number of very large packing crates were removed from Crossmaglen. These had not only made the place look generally untidy and crowded, but because they were on the edge of the Gaelic Football Pitch were a bone of contention with the locals. During my O Group that day, amongst other things, I reminded company commanders that there was no point in having soldiers out on patrol unless that patrol had a specific purpose. There was always the thought that companies would feel that soldiers not out and about were wasting their time, and would consequently aim for an unrealistically high work rate. I stressed that this was the wrong attitude. I also reminded them that the gathering of evidence was their first priority at the scene of a 'find', and everything else should lead to that end product. Finally I cautioned them not to give propagandists the openings they used to such good effect in producing their subversive literature. (For example a soldier in A Company had crept out of the base a few nights before and sawn down a goal post on the Gaelic Football Pitch at Crossmaglen. The locals were, quite reasonably, incensed.)

The funeral of Sergeant Hunter was held at Scarva ten miles away. It was an absolutely typical Ulster funeral of a type which the RUC have seen all too frequently over the last nineteen years. The cortège was formed up behind the coffin and some distance from the church, near the river Bann which was in full spate. It was absolutely teeming with rain, but undeterred the all male cortège proceeded at a very slow dignified and respectful pace uphill through the village to the church which was packed. The RUC officers and I were in dress uniform and without raincoats, and although the procession only took about ten minutes to complete the distance it seemed much longer. We were soaked through to the skin. For me an RUC funeral was a novel event but for many of the RUC officers present and particularly my Chief Superintendent, it was an occurrence re-enacted all too frequently. By 1976 he had already attended scores of similar rites, and by now his total must have risen to three figures. What that does to a man, who sees colleague after colleague laid to rest (especially when some coffins barely contain a few pounds of offal) I do not know, but one can only marvel that in such circumstances there are still men prepared to go about their business impartially, cheerfully and philosophically.

On my return to Bessbrook I found waiting for me a signal from Brigade HQ ordering me to detach one of my platoons to 1 QLR and also requesting the use of the whole of my Patrol Company to carry out a task near Dungannon in the Scots Dragoon Guards area. I reflected wryly that 3 PARA could not be performing too badly; the previous battalion had needed two additional Spearhead Companies to help them cope yet here we were, albeit with a very slightly smaller area, being asked to manage first without the Spearhead Companies, and now without our Patrol Company. The Dungannon task would take, we estimated, about a month, and I was most reluctant to lose my Patrol Company for such a long period. I appealed to the brigade commander, asking him to think again which he did, but found against me.

That evening I went to Crossmaglen to punish the phantom goalpost sawer. A Private, he received 28 days detention (which of course meant loss of pay in addition to imprisonment) to be followed by an administrative discharge from the Army. A harsh punishment for a Public Relations gaffe. If only the Republicans had known how hard we tried to be decent to them.

The following day was an important one. A 'Border Conference' had been convened and was due to start at Bessbrook at 11.20. CLF and the Chief Constable were the principals, with a supporting cast of RUC and Army officers. We started half an hour late and the Chief Superintendent and I both spoke for a few minutes before the Chief Constable outlined his proposals to amalgamate SB, the Criminal Investigation Department, and military intelligence. It sounded well, but I thought he was bound to meet with very considerable resistance not least within the RUC. Then to my utter astonishment the Assistant Chief Constable responsible for the border RUC divisions stood up and stated that cross-border co-operation was good. This was an incredible thing to say for although there was a useful veneer of co-operation at the very lowest working level (for example it was normally possible to get the Garda and the Irish Army to man their side of the border when specifically requested) there was little being achieved at a higher level which gave rise to any optimism. The distinct impression which one got was that the Garda was not actually interested in effecting any improvement. Certainly conciliatory and friendly statements had been issued, but as in so many things actions speak louder than words. Garda action at the time of the SAS incident was typical, and clearly the Garda had taken a smug delight in blowing up a trivial incident into a major international event.

Even on a more routine plane they were obstructionist. Many terrorists on the run from justice in the North were living in Dundalk and the Garda knew most of them. However, our requests for up to date photographs of these people so that we could recognise and arrest them on their occasional sorties into the North, consistently met with a point blank refusal. In terms of the relentless pursuance of terrorists, searching buildings, making arrests, and charging suspects there was all too little sign. Extradition seemed to be a dirty word and the terrorists obviously considered the South to be a completely safe haven in which they could live, plan, manufacture munitions, store weapons and raise money, and from which they could launch their occasional forays into the North, and South Armagh especially.

Fortunately, Kenneth Newman totally disagreed with his Assistant Chief Constable, which saved me from the embarrassment of having to do so myself. Indeed what the Chief Constable desired was something quite visionary, joint intelligence between the RUC and Garda. Nobody in the North would have disagreed with this, but it was way out of reach at that time, although today I understand that it is very much more a reality.

After a pretty quick lunch the Chief Constable and CLF set off by helicopter to visit Forkill and Crossmaglen. Their stay at the former was very valuable, Sergeant Alexander of the RUC giving Kenneth Newman a straight from the shoulder account of their problems in trying to police the area. He also took the opportunity to tell the Chief Constable how counter-productive the SPG could be if they were ever allowed to patrol in the area (as they had been when the previous battalion was responsible).

I remained at Bessbrook Mill that afternoon to mind the shop whilst Andrew took the opportunity to visit 2 and 3 UDR. Once he was back I had time to visit all three bases before dark and then talk to the SAS OC who had just returned from London after seeing the Irish barristers who were dealing with the SAS border incident. He seemed more optimistic about the case.

The 21st and 22nd May were very quiet, so much so that on the 21st I actually got to bed before midnight. On the Saturday evening I went to dinner with the Chief Superintendent and his charming wife in Newry. We had too much to drink (certainly more than the Northern Ireland rule of two pints) and I was in danger of being breathalysed by his own force on my way back to Bessbrook as I was driving myself. He was very interesting on the new Chief Constable – I had not realised until then that although Kenneth Newman had been in the Province for the two previous years he had remained at the RUC HQ in Belfast for much of that time, somewhat insulated from the reality of what life was like out on the ground and especially in the more sensitive police stations and divisions (or certainly that was the unfortunate and probably mistaken impression that he had given).

The following morning I was visited by the two officers from HQNI concerned with press relations. Their office had in the past been accused of manipulating the facts to the advantage of the Security Forces and to the discredit of the terrorists. However, the Army believed that any attempts at propaganda rarely convinced anyone, lacked sophistication and normally backfired. So media policy in 1976 simply meant trying to get the reporters to produce their accounts of incidents accurately and to discourage them from swallowing PIRA's versions with too much haste.

Everyone who has ever been closely involved with a newsworthy event is familiar with the feeling that the media's version is completely unrecognisable, so the job of these press relations officers was to try to get the media's account to bear some resemblance to the truth. In 3 PARA we felt that the Army was very bad at it, although I was personally the first to admit that they had a difficult task. We invariably checked and double-checked our accounts of an event before making a press release, this took time and almost always handed the advantage of immediacy to PIRA. On those occasions when we released before we were absolutely certain of what had occurred we were sometimes embarrassed when we learnt the full story. So normally the terrorists got their version to the media before we did and it was very difficult to refute what was then considered as the authorised account. I left to have lunch in Newry with Support Company, but learnt afterwards that Edward Gardener and others had really lashed into these two over their lunch, perhaps a bit unfairly, and they had left thoroughly chastened.

The guests at Support Company included one person who seemed way right of Genghis Khan. He had been a local Unionist Councillor and he made it abundantly clear that the only way to treat anyone even suspected of terrorism was to kill him and dump him in the sea. He gave the strong impression that most members of the Orange Order had similar sentiments; however like many of the utterances from the more extreme Protestants there was a great deal of bravado but little likelihood that the words would be backed by action. Hot air seemed to be many Protestant politicians' stock in trade.

That afternoon C Company cleared a small landmine (two beer kegs) from one of their border crossings and then a SAS patrol found a wire leading to a culvert just at the point where the main road to Dublin crosses the border (H5). They felt fairly certain that their discovery had not been noticed, and we spent a long time discussing this possible IED. We were very excited; another explosives convoy was due on Tuesday, 25th May, and it was fairly certain that if it was an IED its target would be the convoy, or the escort for it.

Because this might concern the explosives convoy which was a politically sensitive issue our decisions were dependent upon approval from the brigade commander and in principle they were:

To let the explosives convoy approach from the South but then stop it at the border at the last moment.

To plan and send the normal escort from Newry to meet the convoy from the South but stop it just short of the IED and the border.

To insert that evening (23 May) a covert patrol to try to ambush the terrorists who would have to man a chosen firing point and probably lay out more wire.

To photograph, very covertly from the air, the site of the IED (this meant the aircraft had to behave as though it had another task some distance away from the real one).

To plan to carry out a full IED clearance on 25 May after the planned convoy time whether or not we caught terrorists red-handed.

The covert patrol was inserted that evening in anticipation and first thing the following day I flew up to Brigade HQ to discuss the plan with David Anderson. He was in a black mood and was totally against the idea; he said I was to cancel the convoy before it left the factory in the South to avoid any possible risk of it proceeding into the North. Whilst in the area I flew up to Dungannon to see how Roger Miller and his boys were getting on with their surveillance task. They seemed quite happy and were being well looked after which had not been the case when they first went up there. On my way back I diverted to overfly the IED which fortunately was more or less on the direct route between our O'Meath VCP and the Forkill base and then called in at Forkill which was immaculate; I was becoming pretty impressed by the way in which Malcolm was managing both his base and his TAOR.

Next I called in Joe Baker to discuss the IED plan for the morrow; he was most unhappy about it because he thought that the SAS, with my connivance, were taking all the good operations from his TAOR leaving him with solely the routine. In a way he was right, but it was a question of using the best tools for the task in hand and anything that required covert skills demanded the SAS or Patrol Company – and the latter were in Dungannon. However, by 13.30 we had sorted out the various responsibilities and I then tackled Brigade HQ again. This time the Brigadier agreed that we could let the convoy from the South run, diverting it at the last minute to the O'Meath border crossing (H1) instead of the Dublin road (H5). This was not what I had wanted, but it was better than his original decision.

Tuesday dawned and we were all eager with anticipation, but as so often in the past nothing happened, (that is no terrorist appeared in the area of the possible firing point), so we swung into the full IED clearance. This took much of the day and the result was that there had been no IED – just a wire which was a terrible let down. Some consolation was that the operation, involving Support and B Companies in close cooperation with the SAS Squadron, had gone perfectly. Ian Meynell (deputy commander of the brigade) visited all the bases that morning, his first such since we took over from 1 RS. He was amazed at the improved cleanliness, tidiness and general organisation at each place and it was encouraging to know that our efforts were recognised occasionally. At 13.20 after a warning of about 30 minutes a car bomb exploded in central Newry damaging seven shops.

Then at 18.30, horror of horrors, there was another border incursion. This time Sergeant Edwards, with three four man patrols had been briefed to establish a series of short term VCPs at points selected by Colin Thomson. The first was in the vicinity of Coolderry (crossing H25), an area visited by all the men some time previously. The group took off from Crossmaglen and the RAF helicopter pilot initially mistook the chosen drop off point and at 17.50 flew a short distance across the border. He quickly realised the mistake, recovered and dropped the patrols off at the correct spot. As he was alighting Sergeant Edwards noticed a small grey Austin van which, seeing the soldiers, turned round in the road and took another route towards Crossmaglen. Sergeant Edwards immediately, and on the spur of the moment, decided to alter his VCP position to block this other route and he gave his two subordinate patrols new positions to occupy.

One group led by Lance-Corporal Butler was sent closest to the border where he noticed an elderly man beckoning him from the next field. Being naturally curious he went to investigate thinking that the man was in the North. In fact he was just in the South and almost immediately Butler was pounced on by some Garda policemen whom he had not seen

Car bomb in central Newry.

and who presumably had been initially drawn to the spot by the helicopter's inadvertent border overflight. Butler and his patrol were arrested, conveyed to Dundalk and eventually released at 20.50. The familiar nausea followed; a visit by the brigade commander, SIB interviews, reports to Brigade HQ and an exchange of letters. My sympathy lay entirely with Lance-Corporal Butler; he had made a mistake but it was nothing compared with the error made by the helicopter pilot (an RAF Flight Lieutenant) whose error was not criticised by anybody. I wondered whether Brigade HQ would ever learn; their over-reaction to every incident was proving very burdensome.

Wednesday, 26th May, was one of those days one could do without. Andrew had decided to completely change round the Operations Room and this was done overnight. All the built in desks, wiring and lights were moved and chaos still reigned the following morning and the staff there, unused to the new arrangements, were highly critical. However, within 24 hours it was all finished off and most thought the new arrangements more efficient, which they were.

David Anderson came to see me, first to deliver his own personal rocket to Tim Hollis for the Dublin Road incursion, and then to give me a very stern warning that no further incursions could be tolerated. The problem with such a statement was that I certainly did not wish to restrict the movements of either helicopters or patrols but I was clearly on the spot. I confided to my diary 'as usual I can take the major disasters easily but these piddling little problems cause me great mental anguish'. However, I was absolutely determined that my military masters should be more robust and start criticising the Garda's attitude rather than our map reading which in all conscience, given the number of patrols operating day and night close to the border, had been pretty good. This black mood continued the following day but was lifted as I spent much of it discussing and planning the arrangements for 3 PARA's move to Osnabrück from Aldershot (scheduled for the following spring) with the CO of the battalion we would replace there. It seemed a long way ahead but moving 650 men and about 300 families to a new country needed a little forward planning.

My adjutant, Richard Hoyle, and my signals officer, John McPhie, had both tendered their resignations from the Army during the previous three weeks, and not because I was being beastly to them. Richard was disgusted with his next posting, whilst John could see no future in the Parachute Regiment as our brigade was to be disbanded. They each had a point, and I wrote a strong letter to our Regimental HQ in Aldershot to try and save them for the regiment and the Army. They were good fellows and we needed to keep them.

I was obviously feeling pretty frustrated. The SAS Squadron was half way through its tour and apart from Peter Cleary they had achieved no tangible success and we had achieved even less. I wrote down for future reference the seven points which in my view would have helped us to bring the military campaign if not to a halt (only a political change of heart and a cease fire could do that), at least nearer to one. These were:

Proper and effective border co-operation between the RUC and the Garda (including extradition of suspects).
Identity cards.
Cessation of British DHSS facilities for those on the run in the South (their 'dole' could still be drawn in the North).
Death penalty for terrorists who murder.
Detention until the end of hostilities for anyone found guilty of a terrorist offence irrespective of the actual award in court.
Freedom to shoot at armed terrorists without having first to give a verbal warning.
A total ban on provocative marching.

Friday, 28th May, was a fairly uneventful day. I went first thing to Lurgan for the Brigade O Group where the Brigadier gave us all a general rocket but it was not overdone. After lunch I held my own O Group which had been postponed from Tuesday because so much had been happening on that day. Most of the subjects were pretty typical but I did remind the company commanders to be thoroughly conversant with all the regulations contained in a series of aide memoires from HQNI which everyone carried, and the 3 PARA Operation Instruction; to plan and prepare every activity very thoroughly especially when it was close to the border; to be aware that we were having too many 'negligent discharges' – the latter was partly my fault because I had ordered that when patrolling close to the border (that is within a mile or so) all weapons were to be loaded and made ready with a round in the breech and just the safety catch applied.

After the O Group at 15.00 I flew off to look for an unexplained explosion in the Silverbridge area. For the first time I felt really very airsick because the Gazelle had a very bad vibration in the rotor and I was pleased to get safely back to Bessbrook. Then down to Newry for a long chat at the RUC station and on to Support Company.

The weekend was very quiet but not uneventful. Major Kay Coates, a Parachute Regiment officer who was the DAA & QMG (chief administrator) at the Brigade HQ had sent me a questionnaire about Lance-Corporal Butler's incident. I wrote, 'God preserve us from bureaucracy. Life is becoming quite intolerable, I await the delivery of this great document.' It eventually arrived, luckily at the same time as a letter from the CO of 22 SAS who in thanking me for my support for his squadron said:

> This is just a line to say how much I appreciate the way you stood by [the squadron commander] over the cross border incident. It is the sort of thing one expects from a senior officer but regrettably does not always see ... From our point of view I have never known better cooperation between two units than that which exists between your Battalion and D Squadron.

The questionnaire was ridiculous, seeking only a scapegoat. I had no intention of making a sacrifice of Lance-Corporal Butler and I flew to Crossmaglen with the document and gave it to Colin to complete. I asked him to have it ready for the following morning when I was due back at the base for a full scale inspection. In the evening I went out with my rover group to Rostrevor and the O'Meath and Dublin Road VCPs. Everything was very normal, and Rostrevor was in the midst of a Band Festival and bicycle race. I called in at Support Company on the way back where I was fascinated to listen to a tape recording of a PIRA terrorist's ex-girl friend whom we were trying, with some success, to win over as an informer.

My Sunday morning was spent at Crossmaglen conducting a most detailed inspection of the base, looking into every nook and cranny. All in all it was much cleaner and tidier than it had been when we took over, but it still needed some more washing machines; urgent repair to the drainage from the shower and main accommodation blocks; and a new floor in the food preparation room. However, the worst aspect was the canteen which was not very good at all and needed, above all else, a better Pakistani in charge. When I returned to Bessbrook I set these matters in hand before getting down to replying to the Brigadier's letter about Lance-Corporal Butler's transgression. I constructed a reply which I knew would inevitably cause me more trouble, but I felt that I just had to remain loyal to my soldiers and should not ignore the challenge which the questionnaire had thrown down. I noted in my diary that: 'I will live to regret the letter, it's not at all diplomatic but I feel that it must be said.'

The following day, 31st May was theoretically the Whitsun Bank Holiday Monday but that hardly affected us. At 10.30 I went to the new Brigade HQ at Portadown (the Lurgan Knicker Factory had been abandoned) to speak to the deputy, Ian Meynell, about my reply. He looked over my effort and advised me to delete an annex to the letter and a cartoon (David Anderson's sense of humour might not stretch to it). On my return to Bessbrook I redrafted the reply and sent it off after lunch. I include it here, without the annex, which simply answered the questions posed by the questionnaire and was purely factual:

## 3 PARA CROSS BORDER INCURSION 25 MAY 1976

1. The answers to the specific questions posed by Reference B are attached at Annex A. I have discussed the matter in some detail with OC A Company 3 PARA and I am quite satisfied that the correct procedures were followed.

2. I am very worried that the NCO's concerned are to be made scapegoats for a minor error (albeit one with some political connotations) when others are making and have made errors without any hint of revenge. I am quite clear

that neither OC A Company, nor Sergeant Edwards nor Lance-Corporal Butler deliberately or wilfully flouted your orders or mine and if there is any blame to be attached to this incident it is to fall squarely on my shoulders.

3. It was I who as a deliberate act of policy decided that whilst we are in South Armagh we, as a battalion, were going to work hard to get to grips with the PIRA. It was I who decided that Company Commanders were to have autonomy within their own TAOR provided that they worked within the guidelines laid down in 3 PARA Operation Instruction 2/76. It is I who have encouraged Companies not to be absolutely specific about every detail of a patrol commander's task and this was a deliberate policy to discourage pattern setting and to encourage individual initiative.

4. In all of this I have borne in mind the particular qualities of the Parachute Regiment soldier and NCO. Our NCOs are better schooled than NCOs in any other Regiment and are more mature. They should therefore be encouraged to accept a greater degree of responsibility than a line Regiment can expect from its NCOs.

5. I am satisfied that a proper system of briefing and debriefing exists within the Companies but clearly the briefings which soldiers receive cannot be as detailed as those received by members of units with a lower work-rate. A high work rate must inevitably mean that briefing and preparation time is less available, and the problem is striking a balance between over and under briefing.

6. I am very concerned that if petty incidents continue to be blown up out of all proportion that Company Commanders will start to look over their shoulders instead of concentrating their undivided attention on defeating the PIRA. Currently Battalion HQ is partially successful in protecting them.

7. From all of this you may get the impression that I treat the matter of crossing the border lightly. I do not, but I must stress that in the past border incursions have occurred without generating so much steam and although I will do my very best to ensure that there are no more incursions it would help enormously if a more rational view could be taken of genuine mistakes. Where a 'mistake' is a malicious act I will

take appropriate action – for example the soldier who cut down the goal post at Crossmaglen has been awarded 28 days Field Punishment and is being put up for an administrative discharge – but I cannot accept that Officers and NCOs should be punished for genuine mistakes of a minor nature.

8. 3 PARA is here to contribute towards the defeat of the PIRA. We will not begin to do this restricting movement in the Border areas, nor will we defeat them by a welter of protective paper. We can only hope to do it by accepting that soldiers are not perfect. They are people, who given the conditions, luck, leadership, training and encouragement will achieve a modicum of success.

9. So far 3 PARA has taken no casualties. However the whole battalion is well aware that we must expect some and it was made quite clear to everyone before we came that we were going to South Armagh to fight the PIRA offensively. When casualties do occur I hope that we will not be pilloried for adopting this offensive policy.

10. In conclusion therefore I am asked to apportion the blame. The blame is almost entirely mine, I brought them here in the first place and I decided the policy. I have censured the two NCO's concerned but do not feel that more formal disciplinary action against them is appropriate or necessary.

That out of the way I visited Newry, Warrenpoint and Forkill and then, as if to shake all this futile argument out of my system I went for my first run. Round and round the Bessbrook heli-pad and certainly not more than two miles. I was very short of breath and resolved to repeat the performance rather more often in the future. However, there was one more argument with 'authority' before the month ended, and this oddly was with the senior Church of England padre in Northern Ireland. My battalion padre was a super fellow called David Cooper, who was later to achieve renown as the 2 PARA padre in the Falkland Islands. In 1976 his great claim to fame was that he was an international rifle shot. As such he was most unpopular with the Royal Army Chaplains' Department who seemed to think that his shooting ability was a cardinal sin; they therefore made his life more difficult than they did that of any padre I have met before or since.

In Aldershot David took his turn at helping with Services in the Garrison Church but when we were earmarked for Northern Ireland I naturally assumed, as he was our padre, that he would accompany us. My surprise was absolute therefore when I discovered that the senior padre in Aldershot was not prepared to release him.

Eventually after some acrimony my view prevailed, and David came with us. However, I had not been entirely honest because it was my intention that David should return to Aldershot in June to train with my battalion shooting team for the Army's annual inter-unit competition at Bisley which was held in early July, before rejoining us again in South Armagh. But when I came to implement this plan I came across another stumbling block, this time in the shape of the senior padre in Northern Ireland. David had been in Ulster for six weeks and the senior padre there now regarded David as one of his padres and refused to let him return to Aldershot. Knowing that if I won this argument, I would then be faced with an identical contest with the padre in Aldershot in order to get him back for the last four weeks of the tour, I reluctantly conceded defeat. I was in danger of imperilling David's future in the Chaplains' Department but in my view the attitudes of these senior padres was regrettable. They seemed to have little feeling for our difficulties and requirements, my Bisley team went back to Aldershot without him and for David it was another step towards his disenchantment with the Chaplains' Department which he eventually left.

# CHAPTER NINE

# The Propaganda War

As the reader will have seen, during the training period and at every subsequent opportunity I laid great stress on treating the local population with kid gloves, not reacting to provocation and being unfailingly polite, courteous and friendly. Naturally there was a reason for this which went deeper than the ethos behind the Army's role in Ulster. I knew from my previous experience that every Parachute battalion serving in Northern Ireland was subjected to a propaganda war of a higher intensity than that experienced by other battalions. Many people inside and outside the Army and RUC did not understand this and were consequently taken in, at least initially, by much of what they heard. This was unfortunate, because it was an aspect of life which made every Parachute battalion's tour that much more challenging.

The Republican propaganda machine by 1976 was becoming very well refined and it was targeted specifically at those units which made life most difficult for the terrorists. It was natural therefore that 3 PARA's very effectiveness should attract the specific attentions of the propagandists. Regrettably of course, soldiers being soldiers, we sometimes played into their hands and it was child's play for them to blow up every trivial incident at which soldiers had not reacted as perfectly as one would have wished, into vitriolic and nauseating stories. However, most cases of ill discipline or over-reaction in Northern Ireland occur when soldiers are frightened. Those who are frightened tend to bully, but in my 3 PARA I thankfully had very few of these inadequates, and when any were identified they were removed immediately from the patrolling rosters.

All but a fraction of the propaganda was directed against my

Support Company in Newry and Warrenpoint, largely because being in an urban area they had a higher profile and more contact with people. I had given this area to them because Joe Baker, the OC, was familiar with it having very effectively commanded a company there previously. The population of both places was predominantly Nationalist although there were many Unionists living contentedly alongside, particularly in the owner-occupier areas. The housing estates in Newry tended to be almost exclusively Catholic and the worst one, the Derrybeg, although consisting of reasonably modern housing stock, was quite as evil as many of the Belfast estates. In their better days, however, both Warrenpoint and Newry must have been very attractive places.

Warrenpoint, nestling at the landward end of Carlingford Lough, occupies a beautiful site, the scenery is breathtaking and it is situated on the only part of the South Armagh border which is geographically clear with the median line running down the centre of the main shipping channel. It is a deep-water port which has developed into a reasonably thriving container port, the more so during the last decade. Until then a working canal connected Carlingford Lough to Newry but in disuse it has been allowed to decay and the result in central Newry is a stagnant waterway leading to a derelict dockland area.

Newry itself is situated astride the Newry River valley and built up onto the hills which dominate both sides. The shops and business premises are evenly distributed on both sides but with only four bridges across the river Newry was subject to traffic jams. A bomb hoax or security force VCP could all too easily bring the town centre to a complete halt. The older parts of the central town which had been devastated by the bombers over the period 1969-74 were by 1976 slowly coming back to life, and it was a prime concern of 3 PARA and the RUC to see this process proceed as quickly as possible.

In 1973 during my first visit to the area, Newry had given every impression of a Wild West frontier town which to some extent it was. Commercial activity was very restricted and most of the shops were either derelict, boarded up, or poorly stocked. Robberies were frequent, bomb and shooting incidents in the streets were daily occurrences. On that first visit to

Newry I had driven through the town on my way to Crossmaglen in my own mini-van which I had decided would be useful as a covert reconnaissance vehicle. Unarmed and uncertain of the way I stopped at a garage just beyond the infamous Derrybeg Estate to fill up with petrol and to confirm that I was on the right road for Crossmaglen. This request earned me some pretty strange looks and it was only later that I realised that I could perhaps have chosen a safer place to buy fuel.

In 1976 life was being breathed back again into Newry, it was as if the town was waking slowly from a long hibernation, but because of the bridges and the siting of the shops in relation to them it had been impossible to create much in the way of a pedestrian area (a policy which many other Ulster towns had adopted), so the only way to deter terrorists was to keep up a heavy security force presence. By doing this the incident rate could be contained and the town became more and more a place where the inhabitants could feel reasonably safe. There was, however, a heavy penalty. People and vehicles were frequently checked by armed soldiers and police and this is always bound to be irritating particularly for young men in the obvious target group, the 15-25 age bracket. Naturally anyone in a hurry was inconvenienced, and cross words were not an unheard of occurrence. Sometimes, but not often, my soldiers responded in kind, and this was invariably a gift to the propagandists.

Such propaganda was normally confined to the local press (*Armagh and Down Observer, Sunday News, Irish News* and *Belfast Morning News, Newry Reporter*) and most insidious of all the *Republican News* (house newspaper of the PIRA and Sinn Fein) and the *Plough* (South Down/South Armagh's own Republican paper). Few stories were repeated in the more responsible newspapers like the *Irish Times* or *Belfast Telegraph* and hardly any found their way into the mainland press, or the BBC or ITV local or national news channels. The propaganda war was therefore largely a local affair with 3 PARA, the RUC, and the Unionists normally on the same side against the Republicans on the other. This was a most unfortunate polarisation, because we and the RUC were trying to be impartial, although the actions of some Republicans made it very difficult to be or even appear to be totally even-handed.

The active source of most stories was the Republican Club at 1

Trevor Hill, Newry, where the scribe was a fanatic of mainland origin. The convert is always more dangerous than the genuine article and as early as the end of April, less than a fortnight after our arrival, our very effectiveness was causing the first powerful ripples of a virulent campaign against us. The technique used was simple; to take a real incident and alter it, often even to the extent of reversing what actually occurred, to put us in a bad light. This then became the 'fact' of the incident as we did not ever try to contradict such a story even if the editorial staffs had been willing to publish our version.

The first real complaints were voiced at the Newry and Mourne District Council Meeting on 26th Apri'. The Council consisted of both Unionists and Republicans but the criticism came solely from the Republicans and the Social Democrat and Labour Party (SDLP) members who had earlier in the day visited Support Company as a five man delegation. Over the next few weeks the company's behaviour was the subject of considerable discussion within and outside the Council chamber and the amount of column inches in the local press devoted to 3 PARA, and to Support Company particularly, was considerable. Some quotes here will give a flavour of that reporting:

> Workers are daily being stopped, travelling to and from their work places.

> Finally, we would like to explain what the PARAs hope to gain by their terror campaign. They reckon that if they keep this up for the next six months then by that time the people will have got used to it and the RUC will seem like angels compared with the PARAs. In other words the PARAs think that the people of Newry are foolish enough to be tricked into accepting the RUC.

> Members of the Newry and Mourne District Council on 10 May passed a resolution expressing their 'abhorrence at the repressive policy of the 3rd Parachute Regiment and called for an immediate change'. (This resolution was supported by all 9 Republican members, opposed by 5 Unionists with three others abstaining).

> More than a dozen serious incidents have been reported to

Mr Frank Feely, former SDLP Convention member in the last week in which ill treatment took place. In one case PARAs stopped a group of youths returning from a musical session and asked them their religion and age. They were called 'Fenian Bastards' and made to do 36 press-ups.

An allegation that uniformed members of the Army petrol-bombed the shopping centre at the Derrybeg Estate, Newry, has been made by Father Murphy, Sinn Fein Cumann. The Cumann claims that the 'sinister incident' was witnessed by nearby residents.

In Forkill they photographed the whole dole queue, and took their personal details.

Arsonists, bombers and the PARAs condemned.

Since the arrival of the 3rd Parachute Regiment in Newry they have carried out an extensive campaign of harassment and intimidation – statement by the Colman Rowntree Republican Club.

Letters in the *Newry Reporter* of 20 May give three points of view:

### Council Support

Dear Sir, – I was a Para and I was very happy and proud to serve in this fine Regiment, the best in the British Army, and I was very pleased to read in your paper last week that our Council came out to support the job being done by this great Regiment to rid this town of commies and terrorists.

When the British Army came to our fine town they were welcomed by all honest good people here and it was only when the foreign subversives became active that the security forces stuck the boot in, and this was a good job and the people of Newry understand this.

But now the cream of the Army come here the troublemakers quake in their boots and do their best to stir up trouble. They have destroyed the walls of Hill Street with disgusting slogans doubting the manliness of this fine group of men. I am sickened by these slurs at a time when former comrades of the Paras are facing firing squads in deepest Africa for their part in the world struggle against liberation groups and Communism.

PARA AND PROUD

*Bombers – spare a thought for the residents*

Dear Sir, – I would like to say to the bombers and wreckers of houses in Lower Catherine Street and Edward Street could you not spare a thought for the poor unfortunate residents of these dwellings which are in close proximity to the Police Barracks and the Electricity Showrooms? Our houses were badly damaged three or four times recently and three or four times the bombs failed to go off as well.

Now in all fairness to the people living there don't you think we've had enough? We were living in filth and dirt for months on end. Roofs were destroyed, ceilings came down and doors and windows were out and there was rain coming down on all our belongings. In addition during the bomb alerts residents, including children and old people, had to be evacuated several times.

If you, the bomber or perpetrator, were living in our street, close to barracks or to the Electricity Showrooms would you bomb them and have your house destroyed or badly damaged. If your answer is 'yes' then I'd advise you to have your head examined. If your answer is 'no' then I'd say you are a very selfish person. Did it ever occur to you that if you were successful in destroying the Electricity Showrooms or the Barracks they could find alternative accommodation in a very short time, but we, the residents, could not and would have to stay put. What have we done to deserve such treatment?

CONCERNED READER

*Paras treated like neighbours*

Sir, – People of Newry I should like to draw to your attention the harassment we are getting from the Paratroopers in our town. If this is our town why are we letting this happen? We are treating these people like neighbours instead of treating them like the dictators and imperialists that they are. These are the people who are given authority to roam our streets and treat us like dirt. We are the true owners of this land. We are the true Irish. We should be ordering them to do as we wish. I am asking the people of Newry to unite and drive these dictators from our doorsteps. I think, and I am sure that you think that these invaders should be taught a lesson from the humiliated Irishmen of Newry. It is our aim to drive these Imperialist murderers from our Ireland and to establish a social and democratic Republic. I hope this is your aim too.

P.R.O.,
Newry Branch, I.R.S.P.

Much of this criticism died down as it became clear to the people of Newry, including their councillors, that the town was getting fewer terrorist incidents and that life was proceeding towards normality at a faster pace than it had before our arrival. However, the Republican Clubs (whose sympathies were Marxist-Leninist and pro-PIRA) kept up their attacks to the end of the tour. For example at 14.20 on Saturday 24th July a Support Company patrol in the Market area of Newry had one low velocity round (ie from a pistol) fired in its direction and the shot hit a woman in the arm. This was reported in the Republican Club *Plough* as:

On Saturday 24th July around lunch time Newry market was crowded with shoppers. Paratroopers were moving through the market when, without warning, one of them fired off two shots and dropped his rifle. An innocent woman was hit in the arm.

The same publication the following month in an edition which included a long article on the 1846/47 potato famine, and a shorter one on 'dole detectives' also proclaimed its success against 3 PARA:

What has become apparent to us is that, although the PARAs came here with the intention of harassing people, in actual fact, the Republican Clubs have succeeded in harassing the

PARAs to a far greater extent. Baker's phone has not stopped ringing for months and he has become sick of the name Republican Club. He cannot open a paper without seeing his squaddies attacked. A succession of official complaints have been lodged, all of which have been investigated by the Military Police. If nothing else, this creates a great deal of inconvenience and paperwork. On a wider level, it is obvious that this harassment has had a definite effect on the morale of his troops and staff ... A revolutionary organisation does not fight an enemy on the enemy's terms, it attacks the enemy at its weakest points without giving the enemy the chance to strike back.

There in a nutshell was their strategy (not just against us but the RUC as well) yet neither they nor we lost our sense of humour. In the same edition there were signs that, far from Joe Baker having been regarded as an ogre, he was regarded with some affection and respect and quite rightly so too because Newry was unquestionably a more peaceful and pleasant spot thanks to his untiring efforts:

Like everyone else I have spent the last couple of months tripping over the PARAs who are littering our streets. It seems, if my information is correct, and it usually is, that my old friend Major Baker (or Wallaby Balls as he is known to his mates down under in New Zealand) has spent a lot of time trying to look me up. Maybe that would account for his squaddies looking under piles of wood on the building site in Boat Street ...

and

*A Telephone Puts You Closer to Someone*
If you wish to give the Mad Major your personal goodbye and let him know exactly how much you enjoyed his stay, just ring Newry 2736 and ask for him. Sometimes Captain Lewis refuses to let you talk to the Major as he gets jealous but you only have to whisper sweet nothings in his ear and blow him a few kisses and he will do anything for you.

But the most serious attempt to blacken 3 PARA's name was

*Graffiti in Newry.*

made by Father Denis Faul of Dungannon. For years a scourge
of the British Army, Father Faul prepared a 'fact sheet' for
Frank Maguire, Independent MP for Fermanagh and South
Tyrone, to use in the House of Commons at the end of July. It
was excellently printed but the subject matter was pretty
fanciful though paragraph 10 came straight from the heart:

### Repression of the Catholic Minority in Northern Ireland
(Please send abroad to your relatives and the media)
*The Behaviour of the 3rd Parachute Regiment in South Armagh
June-July 1976*

This information sheet was prepared for the use of Frank
Maguire. M.P., in bringing to the attention of the Members
of the House of Commons in London serious allegations and
complaints made against some members of the 3rd
Parachute Regiment (with or without S.A.S. men) during
their operations in South Armagh. Most of the complaints
were notified to the Army authorities and to the R.U.C with
no results as yet. We know of other complaints where the
victims were unwilling to allow the complaint to be made as

the last remark made to them by the soldiers was: 'If you complain about this we will shoot you', and they fear a worse beating if they complain.

The Army is operating with very wide powers under the Emergency Powers Act 1973 and the Prevention of Terrorism Act 1976. Yet again and again we find well founded complaints brought to our attention where some personnell [sic] of the 3rd Parachute Regiment have acted outside the law and ill-treated people, bullied them or threatened their lives. Whether they are doing this with real or tacit permission from their officers is one of the questions Frank Maguire is endeavouring to find an answer to from Roy Mason. M.P.

Respect for law and order and justice is the foundation of peace along with respect for truth. To fight terrorism with terrorist tactics is only compounding the problem and making the task of the peacemaker impossible. One would hope to convince the people, especially the young people, not to be afraid to make their complaints and have them publicised and in this way to achieve fair play and justice. Life for the ordinary Catholic people is being made very difficult and we have had to visit the victims of the actions described in these complaints in General Hospitals and Mental Hospitals where they are receiving treatment as a result of their experiences.

1. Twenty-year-old youth. Taken from his car on June 4th at 10 p.m. at Tamnaghbane on the Camlough-Meigh road while on his way to a dance. Taken to a derelict house, punched and butted and had a gun put to his mouth, life threatened. Taken to Bessbrook, after three hours left at the camp gate to walk home on foot at 2 a.m.

July 7. 8 p.m. Taken from his car at Hugh Byrne's Rise on the Carrickovaddy Road. A knife was thrown at his feet and then put to his throat, given two days to produce information or he would be killed.

July 11. 8.15 p.m. Taken from his car at Carrickovaddy cottages and threatened with death unless he produced information. 'We can get you going to work.'

This youth had to spend over two weeks in a mental hospital receiving treatment after his experience.

2. 21-year-old youth. July 2, working in the hayfield at Carrowmannon; paratroopers made him stand with his hands out, caught him by the throat, put the gun to his ear, made a noise, saying 'You won't hear the real one'.

July 8. 11.30 a.m. taken from the car at Lislea, thumped him in the stomach and kneed him in the back, pulled a lump of hair out of his head, threatened his life: 'The boys who got Cleary will be calling around to see you'. They stole a camera from the car.

July 10. 1.35 a.m. At Silverbridge accompanied by girl friend. Took him from the car to the rear, thumped him on the neck below the right jaw, slapped him around the head, pulled him by the hair, told to open his mouth and a gun inserted; threatened his life; girl friend intervened. Paratrooper said: 'I cut and butchered women in Aden'. They then said: 'If you report this, you'll never see home.'

This youth had to spend a period in hospital for treatment to his mouth which was lacerated.

3. 20-year-old youth. June 25, at 8.05 a.m. stopped with a 20-year-old friend on the Carrickovaddy road while going to work. Taken into a field and made to sit in the nettles and turn on my nose and mouth in the nettles; hit me in the belly with his fist; put the gun to my head and threatened to shoot me; took my sandwiches from the car and eat them and took a packet of cigarettes; interfered with the car so that it had no brakes.

Another day they made us lie on our backs in the field for an hour; when we refused to sing: 'God Save the Queen' they made us run up and down with their heavy radio pack on our backs.

4. July 7, 7.45 p.m. on the Carrickovaddy road two Paratroopers exposed themselves to an old woman and a young girl.

5. July 10, a worker alleged that £40 was stolen from his coat at a road block near the Mountain House.

6. July 18, 18-year-old youth held for an hour at a road block at 2 p.m. Thumped and kicked in the stomach. Then examined his stomach to see if there were any marks.

7. June 24. 21-year-old youth. Arrested and taken to Bessbrook at 10.15 p.m. Blackmailed with threat of re-arrest

if he did not turn informer.

8. June 22. Two 17-year-old youths arrested in Newry; obscene suggestions made to them about their Catholic girl friends.

9. Easter Monday, 18th April. 26-year-old man arrested at Killeen, taken to Bessbrook, thumped and kicked and threated [sic] and blackmailed.

10. Harassment of priests by long holdups at roadblocks and illegal questioning.

Despite all this we were not losing our sense of humour. Since about the second week of the tour an amusing broadsheet called *Backblade*, whose trademark was an officer with a dagger firmly implanted between the shoulder blades, had been enjoyed throughout the battalion, especially by the officers and NCOs. The editorial staff, principally two young officers who devoted their spare time to it, took great pleasure in taking a dig at anyone who had made a nonsense, or whose behaviour could be ridiculed in any way. Certainly it was popular, and many members of the battalion returned with copies in their scrap books as I discovered whilst gathering material for this account.

# CHAPTER TEN

# Success and Failure

## *1st-30th June 1976*

June 1976 was to prove sunny, exceptionally dry and reasonably uneventful. Apart from a number of hoax bomb warnings and suspicious cars the first week was almost incident free. That did not, however, mean that work stopped, it meant simply that what was planned could proceed almost without interruption.

R and R was by now well under way and Andrew Dudzinski returned from his as Richard Hoyle departed. In that way we were consistently short-handed throughout the two months which spanned the R and R programme. However, we did increase our strength by one, for Pat Conn, having recovered sufficiently from his back injury, returned to work and service with the battalion until September, when he was due for posting to the MOD. I was delighted to see him back to duty and spent some time with him discussing his future employment. I intended to keep Andrew as operations officer, a job which he was doing quite superbly, and put Pat to coordinating our Intelligence and hopefully remedying some of the problems in that area. Intelligence was in any case his first love.

At 11.00 I went to Newry for my formal inspection of Support Company. They had made terrific progress during the past six weeks, and the whole ambience had improved unrecognisably. I was very pleased, and pleased also on my return to Bessbrook to be met with a message from Brigadier David telling me, in reaction to my Lance-Corporal Butler letter, that I owed him a whisky. He had let me off lightly, yet the following day his HQ sent out a new instruction about operating close to the border which was nothing more than another umbrella. My views on the brigade commander were becoming quite confused; I liked him very much and most of the time he seemed very relaxed, but the over-reaction which followed these pettifogging incidents seemed uncharacteristic. Maybe he was just passing on instructions from HQNI who in their turn were probably also under pressure from London.

The following day we nearly suffered an unnecessary fatality. I was out at dusk with my landrovers on the Warrenpoint Road, and with Joe Baker's group we set up a joint VCP on the dual carriageway close to the point where three years later 2 PARA, then commanded by Colin Thomson, were to lose eighteen men, killed in two explosions. It was a fairly straight piece of road yet an MG 1100 saw us too late, streaked across the central reservation (narrowly missing two soldiers who were lying there) crossed the opposite carriageway and crashed into a brick wall. The driver was fortunately uninjured.

The Brigade O Group on 4th June was the first to be held in the new HQ at Portadown which was clearly going to be a significant improvement on the Knicker Factory. It was clean, airy and bright with plenty of space – all things which were absent at Lurgan. Portadown was also closer to Bessbrook which for me was an advantage.

Over the weekend I finished off my round of inspections with B, C and HQ Companies. Everywhere there had been significant improvements over the weeks since we took over and I was content that whatever else we handed to 40 Commando, we would be fitting them into a much better series of bases than we inherited. On Sunday, 6th June, my new RSM arrived. Mr Campbell, the departing RSM, had been very good for me and the battalion. He was a soldier of the old school with high standards, an imposing stature, and a great affection for 3 PARA and its soldiers, who in their turn held him in high regard. I was pleased that I was able to get him appointed MBE before he finally retired – he had devoted his whole life to the Parachute Regiment and much of it had been spent in 3 PARA. His replacement, Mr MacDonald, was of a different era and had not served with 3 PARA previously. He was to have his work cut out to gain the affection, confidence and respect that his predecessor had enjoyed throughout all ranks in the battalion.

Monday, 7th June, was a typical day. At 10.30, Patrol

Company, who were back at last from their task at Dungannon, called for a helicopter to pick up a patrol which had captured a wanted man. The LS was two fields from the border, but the pick up proceeded smoothly and the man was brought back to Bessbrook. There it was rapidly established that he was not a wanted man at all and that the SB information, upon which Patrol Company had been basing their activities, was inaccurate so he was released after being questioned. This was an example of something which occurred all too often; some of my men would spend days trying to identify and catch a wanted man who would then be cursorily interviewed by SB and released.

I was due to visit HMS *Alert* that morning, but before I went I encountered Brigadier David who had already been to Crossmaglen. After visiting *Alert*, I went there myself to discuss tactics for trapping the PIRA. We had been developing the idea for some time of running a fake discotheque at Crossmaglen on Saturday nights. The idea was to have the music, the girls, the absence of soldiers from town patrol, and the late start on the Sunday in the hope that PIRA would genuinely think that we had dropped our guard. The reality was to be that every route out of Crossmaglen would be covertly ambushed and a large reaction force was to be ready in Crossmaglen for instant action. After seeing Colin Thomson I went to Malcolm Cuthbertson to sort out a nonsense which had occurred during the weekend when a UDR company operating in his area had very nearly had a shoot out with the SAS. I concluded that Malcolm was probably at fault and I made it plain to him that when dealing with the UDR it was very dangerous to assume anything. They needed a much more detailed briefing than was customary for our more highly trained regular soldiers.

Returning to HMS *Alert* to pick up a signaller I had left with them to try and sort out their radios (which were often troublesome due to salt air corrosion) we flew low over the mud flats. Duck, cormorants, gulls, terns and small waders were there in abundance. A pleasant sight and I was sad that I could not take the time off to watch them for a while.

After dinner that evening we had a little 'Council of War' – the SAS squadron commander, Roger Miller, Pat Conn, Andrew and the IO – to decide what to do next. We considered four possibilities:

> The Disco at Crossmaglen.

> Siting a permanent OP to overlook the Border Inn on the main Dublin Road border crossing (H5).

> Moving the mobile Dublin Road VCP to a more permanent site.

> Continuing with the lure type operation of the previous fortnight (Operation Pike).

We did not discuss covert patrols or OPs on specifically targeted people, these underlay all our actions anyway and we needed no convincing that they could individually or severally prove useful. Rather it was the more overt activities designed to catch or induce a full-scale PIRA attack (coat trailing). After a long discussion we decided to pursue the first two.

The following day was the normal Tuesday of meetings but with a difference. The HSB and I agreed that we would start a weekly intelligence meeting which was a major breakthrough and a sign that the thaw, following Pat's arrival, was beginning. Then in the afternoon I attended the LSC meeting, this time held at Kilkeel in County Down. It was, for a reason which I never fully learnt, boycotted by the SDLP so all the motions were favourable to 3 PARA for a change. One subject which the councillors had been asked for an opinion on by the Northern Ireland Office, was whether or not the death penalty should be reintroduced for terrorism. Those attending, being all Unionists, had no doubts!

There was one unusual incident during the day: at 07.15 a brown and white Austin Cambridge car owned and driven by James Kearley of Forkill was hi-jacked by ten armed men just north of H17. The driver was hooded and held in an unoccupied house in the Republic south of H17 until 09.35 when he escaped and made his way to the Forkill RUC Station where he reported the incident at 10.00. Meanwhile at 09.20 two gunmen entered Fishers Coal Yard at the Albert Basin in Newry. In the yard office John Heasley of 3 UDR was hit by nine bullets; his workmate Don Littlewood also received several gunshot wounds and Dennis O'Hagan was injured by flying glass. All were taken to the Daisy Hill Hospital Newry. O'Hagan was released that day, Littlewood a few days later, and miraculously even Heasley eventually recovered.

The gunmen escaped down the Dublin Road in the car and at 09.50 it was stopped by the Garda just north of Dundalk where one officer was shot in the knee and another suffered from shock. One gunman was recognised by them as a Dundalk resident and the car was eventually found abandoned just south of H17. It was a classic example of an incident pattern repeated all too frequently in Ulster over the last few years – the unusual element on this occasion was the shooting of a member of the Garda.

Julian Thompson (40 Commando RM) arrived with the whole of his reconnaissance party on that day and I gave them a full briefing. It was a sure sign that we were well into our tour. The following day I took Julian around all the bases and then at 21.15 a patrol from Patrol Company caught two members of the Garda on our side of the border by the railway (H9). They were unarmed and we requested further instructions which came 15 minutes later, personally from the Brigadier, to release them. We attempted to arrange a press release but the CLF would have none of it. According to the BBC an Irish Army football team travelling from Castleblaney to Dundalk also crossed into the North that day, but we did not see them. For Patrol Company this was the third time in three days that their patrol close to the border had carried out an arrest and in the process compromised their OP position. It was a clear hint that they should withdraw from that area for quite a while.

Thursday, 10th June, was the last day of the 40 Commando RM reconnaissance which had turned up no serious problem areas. After they had departed I held my weekly O Group which included cautionary points on changing the types and times of administrative vehicle journeys and avoiding derelicts (many of which had been known to be booby-trapped).

The following morning at 06.45 I departed for my R and R. This was a blessed break and a time to renew my acquaintance with my three daughters, with Paddy and to do something quite different from soldiering for a few days. I returned refreshed to Bessbrook at 23.00 on Tuesday, 15th June. Two things had happened whilst I was away – both serious.

The first occurred at 23.15 on Saturday night and I learnt

about it the following morning when Edward telephoned me at home just before I heard of the incident on BBC Radio 4. The story was that an eight man patrol from C Company had been working along the road which runs from Meigh through Drumintee to Forkill from early afternoon, carrying out occasional VCPs and in between lying still to watch the road. Their frequency of VCPs increased as the sun set and between 22.00 and 23.15 they had conducted several and moved about 1000 metres along the road during that period. At 23.15 there was a loud explosion which occurred level with the rear end of the patrol. The patrol commander ran back and was relieved to find that although some of his men had been hurled to the ground none was seriously injured. As the dust of the explosion cleared he saw a car with headlights full on stopped on the Meigh side of the explosion area.

Precisely what happened next was never one hundred percent clear. Many of those present had received a considerable shock and some had been physically blown off their feet by the force of the explosion. It was dark and the first thing that everyone seemed to recall was that looking back towards the area of the explosion they were blinded by the headlights of a car. The patrol commander shouted at this car to turn its headlights off but hardly surprisingly those in the car, a Ford Cortina driven by Carol Lavery of Tandragee and containing five others, did not hear him. Two soldiers were quickly despatched the 60 metres to the car to get the driver to comply.

As they reached the car, another was approaching from the direction of Meigh so as the Ford Cortina switched off its lights the second car, a Triumph driven by Liam Prince of Warrenpoint, slowed down behind it. To the other members of the patrol it must have seemed that the headlights of the first car remained on, but in fact its dazzling effect was replaced by that of the Triumph. For some inexplicable reason, but probably impulsive fright, Prince suddenly accelerated past the Ford Cortina and one of the two soldiers who were by it fired one shot in an attempt to bring it to a halt. To the other members of the patrol it must have seemed that the shot came from the Triumph, and two other soldiers opened fire killing the driver. This was a most unfortunate tragedy.

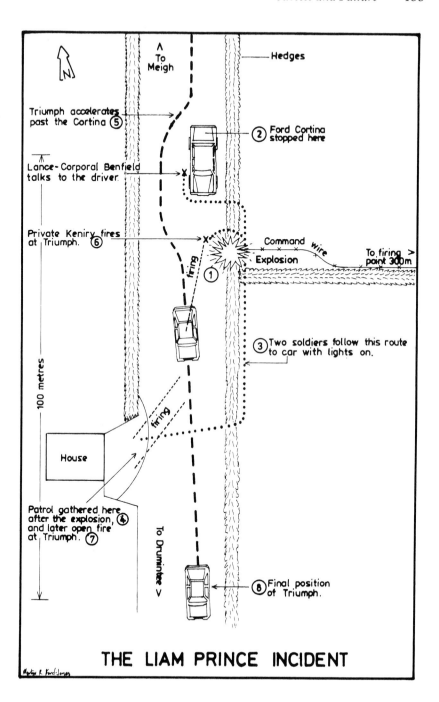

**THE LIAM PRINCE INCIDENT**

FIRING
POINT

*The Liam Prince incident: the firing point (above), and the view from the firing point to the target (below).*

LOCAT
OF DEVIC

COMMAND
WIRE

*The road and command wire (above), and the location of the bomb (below).*

The PIRA had caused the explosion, which consisted of 200 lbs of home made explosive detonated by command wire, so the terrorist must have been within a few hundred metres at the moment of the attack. Clearly such an amount, detonating in the dark, caused considerable disorientation, even to those who were not physically damaged by the device. Liam Prince, driving innocently along a road which he must have known was not entirely safe from terrorism, probably panicked when he saw the armed men by the first car, almost certainly suspecting that they were terrorists and not realising they were soldiers. We can only speculate on the thoughts that went through his head but my deepest regret was that we had killed an innocent civilian and, because the case had become sub judice, I was not able to express my sympathy and regret to his parents, who very reasonably were extremely bitter, and not unnaturally accused us of organising a 'cover up'.

For myself I would place the blame fairly and squarely on the PIRA. Certainly, with hindsight my soldiers made a tragic error, but it was one which was very easy to make in the circumstances. Their split second reactions in the aftermath of an explosion which could so easily have killed a number of them, should not be subject to cold analytical appraisal in slow time. The DPP presumably thought so also, for he decided that prosecution would be inappropriate.

The second incident had in point of fact, occurred the previous week, on 6th June, but had only just come to light and Brigadier David Anderson was on the telephone to tell me about it almost as soon as I arrived back in Bessbrook at 23.15. It seemed that in winding up their operation at Eglish, near Dungannon, my Patrol Company had taken it into their heads to place sandbags over the heads of the men they arrested. Why they did this was always a complete mystery and was never satisfactorily explained during the subsequent enquiries, for it was an action which was expressly forbidden in Northern Ireland (although perfectly normal in training for General War) and the nausea which it caused was to undo much of the good will which their month's work in the area had accumulated.

But worse, in my view, was the way in which the matter had come to light. Their transgression had been reported to the

Brigadier by one of the two groups who had in the first instance, and against my wishes, persuaded the Brigadier to order me to detach the company for the task, namely the Scots Dragoon Guards, and the RUC in Dungannon (I was never quite certain which). I was not amused and naturally, I was very cross with Patrol Company but was almost speechless at the lack of loyalty which had been displayed towards the company who had, after all, been working for another RUC police division and were under command of the Scots Dragoon Guards. The innuendo which they managed to create was that the actions were typical of 3 PARA, when more realistically it should have been perceived that their ill discipline was at least partly due to a lack of control and detailed instructions on their part. Whichever way one looked at it, it was not a good way to be welcomed back to Bessbrook.

I quickly settled back into the routine. During 16th June I managed to visit each company and the RUC Station and was in turn visited by Brigadier David Anderson and Colonel Ian Meynell. There was a tremendous feeling of frustration abroad which I shared, for I wrote in my diary that night, 'Please God give us that break we really do need.' For an agnostic to write that, things must have been getting a bit desperate!

Before going on my R and R Roger Miller and I had agreed that we were putting many of his men in danger by trying to keep a covert watch on the Border Inn at Flurrybridge almost continuously. This was a public house in the Republic but situated on the main Dublin Road and just a hundred yards from the border and often frequented by 'on the run' terrorists from the North. We decided therefore to construct an obvious OP (nick-named Firebase Miller) on the hill which overlooked the inn and which we could use in relative safety. This would then make it easy for us to watch those using the inn, and enable us to photograph them using large 500mm telescopic lenses.

More interestingly, however, we thought the base might attract sufficient attention to incite an attack, and we decided to site it with this in mind. So during my leave, work had been started and a huge quantity of sandbags was helicoptered to the chosen spot to make a solid position (digging was out of the question as the ground was rock under the thin top layer of peat).

The Brigadier unfortunately got to hear of our construction work and on Friday, 18th June (Waterloo Day), when I attended his O Group he informed me that he was totally against such a permanent post, a principle which I agreed with myself. But he refused to accept any of the excellent arguments in favour of making an exception in this instance and demanded that I dismantle it. My first reaction was to try and turn it into some sort of ambush but on further thought I decided that it would be best to cut our losses and I ordered that it be removed – for the time being.

At 16.00 Enoch Powell visited again, this time accompanied by the Earl of Warwick. Mr Powell was in very good form, but my only record of our conversation is that I asked him to support the desire for identity (ID) cards. This was an old chestnut but in Northern Ireland we had the most ridiculous situation that we were always stopping people and asking them to prove their identity but there was no common means by which this was done. Driving licences, Department of Health and Social Security (DHSS) cards, and credit cards were the currency of this game – how much more efficient it could have been if everyone carried an ID card with a photograph. At 17.00 I visited Malcolm Cuthbertson at Forkill and on my way back flew over Firebase Miller which was nearly dismantled. Such a pity.

Saturday, 19th June, was a day of considerable depression. I first visited the two C Company soldiers who were still in hospital following the explosion the previous weekend. They were making excellent progress and were due for release the next week. Then I called at RUC Newry where I had a drink with the Chief Superintendent and thereafter visited Colin Thomson and then Joe Baker. But it was not these meetings which caused my depression, rather it was the weight of bureaucracy which was bearing down on me. I wrote:

> Feel very jaded today, in fact everyone seems to be afflicted by the same problem. Everything we do is wrong. We are simply not being allowed to decide upon a course of action and get on with it. I don't really know who is to blame, London, Lisburn or Brigade. I suspect a bit of each but whichever way we look at it we are being hampered,

**Above** *Firebase Miller. In this view, the Border Inn on the Dublin Road is left centre and Flurrybridge is in the centre. Northern Ireland is in the foreground.*

**Below** *Sergeant Fenwick at Firebase Miller.*

deterred, discouraged and indeed stopped from going for the PIRA. One simply cannot help being disloyal when everyone above is trying like hell to bring some 3 PARA soldiers to trial. No one seems to mind about the PIRA at all. Rules, regulations, inhibitions are quoted one after another to encourage us to stay in barracks but we bloody well will not. We are going to pursue our policy of going out to get PIRA.

The mood quickly lifted and on Sunday, 20th June, I spent a delightful five hours on patrol with Richard Gash, one of my youngest subalterns, in the border area south-east of Forkill. It was pleasantly warm, the gorse was in full bloom and the countryside hummed with the buzz of insects and enthusiastic chirping of the birds. A lovely day for a walk in the countryside. The patrol was very well controlled moving in excellent multiples of four men making intelligent use of the ground and looking extremely alert. It was a joy to see them working as a well oiled machine. For myself, I felt like an old man, creaking somewhat and decidedly unfit; I was glad that unlike the soldiers I was not carrying much kit.

On my return I visited two parades in Newry (one Catholic and one Protestant Orange Order) before going back to Bessbrook to catch up on the paperwork. The first letter I opened was the SIB's preliminary report on Patrol Company's efforts at Eglish which had been gleaned from the evidence of those arrested. It made a very strong case against them, though I thought that Roger would come out of it all unscathed. I resolved in any event that I would support him absolutely because his only 'crime' was a burst of over-enthusiasm.

Christopher Ewart-Biggs, the new British Ambassador in Dublin, visited Bessbrook at 14.30 on Tuesday, 22nd June. He was a charming man and the points which I stressed to him were:

1. The Republican nature of South Armagh.

2. The significance of the border in that the terrorists live across it, that weapons and explosives are stored there, and the Garda have not provided us with up to date photographs of wanted men.

3. Cooperation between the RUC and Garda was more in the desire than the fact.

4. That border incursions were bound to occur.

At 17.23 an event for which we had all been waiting apprehensively occurred. A twelve man patrol from A Company commanded by the previously mentioned Sergeant Edwards had been deployed to the Cullyhanna area the evening before on a 36 hour task. Their first job had been to talk to certain local residents and to photograph the border crossing points H36 and H37. At about 15.45 the patrol was in the vicinity of Teer near H35, a particularly quiet and unpopulated part of the border. Lance-Corporal Butler's section was told to reconnoitre a helicopter landing site about 400 metres away which he did. This pick-up point was confirmed to A Company HQ by radio in code, and the whole patrol then moved to secure the site so that they could be airlifted to Cullaville to begin another task.

In the process of securing the site the two groups commanded respectively by Corporal Tobin and Lance-Corporal Butler had to negotiate a typical South Armagh blackthorn hedge which was atop an earth bank and interlaced with barbed wire. Butler's section successfully crossed this obstacle which was clearly visible to the Republic some 1000 metres away and were followed by Tobin's. As Tobin was crossing there was a devastating explosion which blew him into the field. Basically uninjured he picked himself up and called to his other three men and it quickly became apparent that two were injured whilst the third, Private William Snowdon who had caught the full force of the treacherous device, was in a very bad way indeed. Corporal Tobin initiated a radio call for assistance and it was not many minutes before a helicopter arrived from Bessbrook to fly all three men to the Army's Musgrave Park Hospital in Belfast.

Fearing that there could easily be more devices in the area (a common PIRA tactic) caution was then the order of the day – indeed I remember becoming very irritated by our two explosives experts who were being ultra cautious which necessitated A Company keeping guard of the area throughout the night so that a full clearance operation could be mounted the following day.

On hearing of the outrage, Brigadier David Anderson visited. Until then it had been a good day for him for he had learned that he was very deservedly to be honoured by the award of a CBE in the Birthday Honours. He first visited Crossmaglen to commiserate with Colin but finding no one in, came on to Bessbrook. When he had departed I re-visited the scene of the incident again. I persuaded Colin to return to Bessbrook leaving the task of guarding the area to a platoon commander and took the two explosives experts back to Bessbrook with me. This ensured that the three people who needed to make sound decisions the following day had a good night's sleep. At Bessbrook I concluded my argument with the explosives experts giving in gracefully myself for it was their lives which would be at risk the following morning, not mine.

My first reaction had been to question why it had happened, and in particular whether A Company had committed the ultimate sin of setting a pattern of activity by using the same routes regularly or frequently. I was reassured by Colin that this was not the case; indeed A Company had complied strictly with my orders which were that after each patrol the patrol commander was to plot his exact route on a master map kept by the company and that before each patrol the patrol commanders in planning their routes were to consult the map and avoid areas which had been visited previously. This of course was more easily said than done, but in the case of the hill on which young Snowdon was blown up it had only been visited once before during our two and a half months there. What was much more likely was that PIRA had speculatively inserted a bomb in the embankment at a point where it was easiest to get across for although one told and taught patrols not to use gaps it was unrealistic to expect them to batter their way through every hedge, because as these occurred at very short intervals progress on foot would have been snail like. The PIRA would then have been alerted each time an Army patrol appeared in the area, hoping against hope that their chosen gap would be used by the patrol.

The following day, 23rd June, A Company spent all day winding up the aftermath of the explosion which turned out to

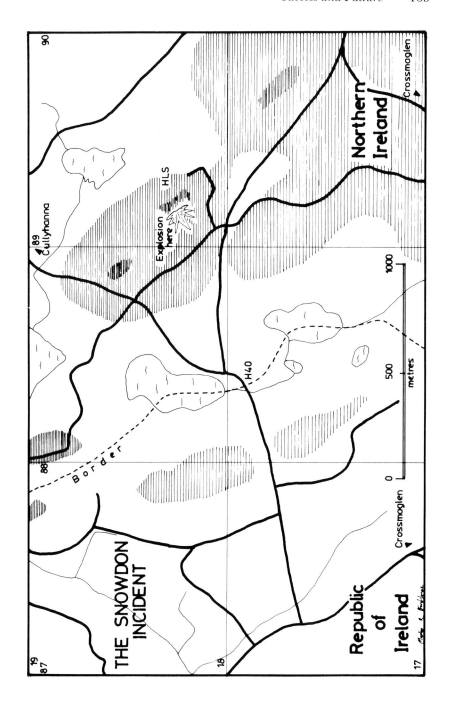

THE SNOWDON INCIDENT

Border

Cullyhanna

Explosion here

HLS

Northern Ireland

Crossmaglen

Crossmaglen

Republic of Ireland

H40

metres

0        500        1000

have been a solitary device consisting of 40 lbs of commercial explosive triggered by radio control. Bomb intelligence collected some useful information including the knowledge that the radio receiver had been fitted with a self-destructing mechanism, and in process poor Snowdon's rifle was found in little pieces some way away from where he had lain. Having seen the rifle it was not difficult to understand the damage that he must have suffered himself and later in the day he was transferred to the Royal Victoria, the civilian hospital in Belfast.

A Warrant Officer of the RMP SIB arrived at 09.00 to conduct the full enquiry into the Eglish affair by interviewing the soldiers. I took an immediate dislike to him and I wrote that 'his interrogation of the soldiers was very stiff, they were not allowed to remain silent and in our view he treated them with far less respect than we had treated the prisoners we were accused of mishandling.' I was very very cross about the whole thing.

At about 10.30 A Company was presented with an opportunity to even their score with the PIRA. A patrol led by Sergeant Lucey did well and sighted two gunmen who had clearly not seen him. Uncharacteristically, because he was an absolutely first class soldier, he then opened fire at the excessive range of 600 metres with a machine gun, but not unnaturally at that distance the 30 rounds were wasted and the gunmen made good their escape. This was really irritating, the siting was about four kilometres from the border and had Lucey acted differently, we would have had an ideal opportunity to cut off their escape route using the helicopter borne ARF. Eventually, after fire had been opened the ARF and QRF were deployed but it was then far too late to prevent the terrorists regaining the sanctuary of the Republic.

It was a dismal day. I was cross with the RMP SIB, irritated by Lucey's failure, sad about Snowdon and I was finding myself isolated from my superiors and my own officers and men all at the same time. I resolved that the following day I would spend as much time out of Bessbrook as I could, but so much for good resolutions, the SIB still conspired to annoy. They had been due to return to Bessbrook to recommence interviews at 10.00 and to that end we brought some men especially in from patrol

*The Snowdon incident: the direction of travel (above), and his rifle (below).*

and then woke them ready for 10.00. Just at 10.00 the SIB Warrant Officer rang to say that he would not arrive until 11.30. This thoughtlessness served only to reinforce the very poor opinion which we in 3 PARA had of the RMP who seemed to us to be tactically inexperienced, arrogant and biased. I thought it prudent to leave on my rounds, all the bases and the Newry RUC station, before he and I had an argument.

Late in the afternoon we did something right. At 16.35 we stopped a white Transit van with false number plates containing three suspected terrorists from Crossmaglen. In the van were two toy pistols and a strong smell of explosive. They were handed over to the RUC in mint condition. This cheered us up and a couple of complaints, one from the RUC and another from our bête noire the Republican Club, were just shrugged off and we spent a pleasant evening at Bessbrook chatting to two visitors, Major Hew Pike (who was to command 3 PARA in the Falkland Islands several years later) and Major Sandy Lindsay, the previously mentioned chief of NITAT.

On Friday I attended the usual O Group at Brigade Headquarters and afterwards received my usual half rocket from David Anderson – this time supposedly about an RUC SPG patrol which one of mine had 'arrested' the previous week. He wanted a complete report on the incident which I accomplished in record time as it was very easy to do so; the SPG had been in completely the wrong place and not unnaturally aroused suspicion.

In the evening I drove down to Newry with my rover group. We had to pass the Derrybeg estate where it had been rumoured that several people were waiting to petrol bomb passing patrols. Unfortunately none materialised. On arrival at Support Company I learnt that Joe Baker would be out until 22.15 but at 22.00 the electrifying news came across on the vehicle radio that Colour-Sergeant Baughan had ambushed four gunmen near the Mountainhouse Inn (halfway between Bessbrook and Newtownhamilton). It was a case for instant action. I ordered Major Roger Miller to take my Gazelle helicopter, which was at Bessbrook, and the ARF whilst I made my way at best speed to the area by road, a distance of about seven miles.

We arrived close to the scene in record time but I didn't want to get too enmeshed in the action until I was quite clear about who was where. It was still reasonably light as complete darkness, just four days after the summer solstice, does not really arrive until nearly 23.30 in Ulster. Roger up in the Gazelle gave me a quick run-down on the situation. Colour-Sergeant Baughan had seen the four armed terrorists moving across country towards the main road. He was worried that unless he took some rapid action they would disappear, so having called for reinforcements he opened fire on the party at a range of about 300 metres. The terrorists scattered and no hits were claimed but when he arrived above the scene a few moments later, Roger Miller spotted two terrorists running away to the east. He was able to get the QRF landed close by and the two men were seen to enter a bungalow.

With my landrover I rapidly took up a position blocking the main road about 500 metres east of the bungalow ostensibly to prevent the terrorists breaking that way. Imagine my surprise, therefore, when a few minutes after our arrival the parish priest from neighbouring Camlough village drove up and asked to be allowed up to the bungalow; apparently the terrorists had telephoned him in the hope that he would be able to reach them before we did. But for the freak chance that my vehicles were blocking the road he would have succeeded, to what effect one could only speculate. While this was happening the QRF under Lieutenant Simon Barry, a young subaltern from B Company, had surrounded the bungalow where the terrorists held an elderly couple hostage. Rapidly assessing the situation Simon quickly called a warning and then fired a couple of rounds through the front room window and up through the ceiling. This had the desired effect and the two gunmen immediately surrendered.

One interesting aside to all this was the attitude of the elderly couple who had been held hostage. Apart from the broken window and shot hole in the ceiling their bungalow was undamaged but their hate for us, and their support for the armed youths, was very poignant, an intense tribal loyalty which defied morality.

So far so good, but where were the other gunmen? By this time many more of my men had reached the area and a patrol from B Company found the gunmen's car (a Peugeot 504

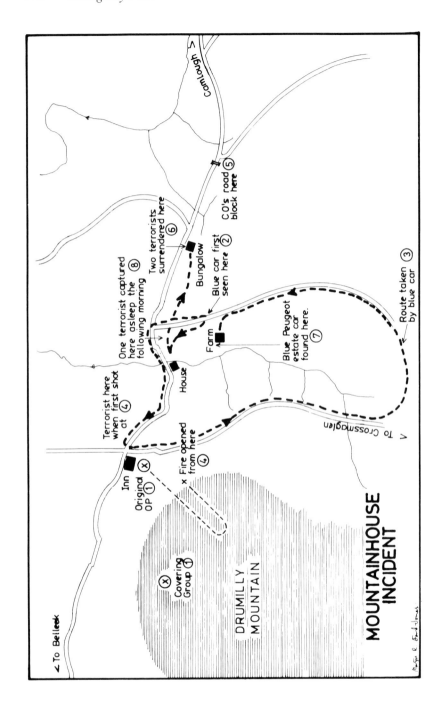

To Belleek

Camlough

CO's road
block here (5)

Two terrorists
surrendered here (6)

One terrorist captured
here asleep the
following morning (8)

Blue car first
seen here (2)

Bungalow

Terrorist here
when first shot
at (4)

House

Farm

Blue Peugeot
estate car
found here. (7)

To Crossmaglen

Route taken
by blue car (3)

Inn

Original (1)
OP (X)

x Fire opened
from here (4)

Covering (X)
Group (1)

DRUMILLY
MOUNTAIN

MOUNTAINHOUSE
INCIDENT

which had been hijacked some hours earlier) together with a Sten gun, but there was no sign of the remaining two terrorists. With the light failing fast there was nothing much we could do except swamp the area with troops overnight and resume the search in the morning. Morning dawns early (at about 03.00) and when the route that the terrorists had taken was retraced a third man was found asleep under a hedge with an Armalite cradled in his arms (at a point where I had walked with my RSM the previous night), but there was no sign of the fourth man. However, reports later indicated that a man from the area had been admitted to the Dundalk Hospital with gunshot wounds in his back.

That was the story as it was revealed in the heat of the moment. The full story differed significantly at a number of points and it is probably worth explaining in detail here, not least because the action was considered a superb example of quick reaction, excellent cooperation between soldiers of different companies, and invaluable helicopter flying. We considered ourselves particularly fortunate that Major Tim Taylor, the Army Air Corps squadron commander, and a great pilot in whom we had total trust, was on duty in my Gazelle that evening.

So, back to the beginning. Colour-Sergeant Baughan's original task had been to watch the Mountainhouse Inn (which had attracted the attention of a recent routine patrol and was also the scene of a shooting incident on 23rd April) and to take photographs of those using the establishment. He was using the normal patrol strength of four including himself in the OP, and a further four in a supporting role. The selected site for his OP was only 30 metres from the inn, whilst the back-up party were on the northern side of Dromilly Mountain (not really a mountain, just a hill). Both positions had been occupied at 03.30 and in the OP Baughan had spent a useful day taking photographs and noting movements.

However, their position must have been poorly concealed for at 17.35 a young boy approached their hide and clearly saw the party. In South Armagh young children are frequently used to search for covert OPs as they can do so without arousing too much suspicion and without getting arrested as an adult male might. Anyway, in this instance they had certainly been compromised and three hours later Baughan evacuated the OP and moved onto the high ground. Leaving his radio operator (Private McCallum) and his gunner (Private Bourne) in a secure place he set off with the other member of his group, Lance-Corporal Jones, to try to find a new OP site. By then the time was 21.00. They moved cautiously as it was still very light, taking time to observe the area in detail. At about 21.25 Baughan noticed four men getting out of a blue estate car which was parked some 500 metres from his position on a minor road, all four were armed and hooded. Using hedgerows for cover the quartet moved northwards and arrived at the house on the main road where two of them were seen to talk to some people in the backyard. Meanwhile a fifth man who had remained in the car drove off at high speed on a circular route which took him past the house, where he collided with a parked vehicle, up to the inn where he turned south to eventually work in his way back to his start point where he parked the car in a garage of a small farm. He was not seen again.

Having left Bourne with the Light Machine Gun (LMG) further up the hill, Baughan was concerned that he had too little firepower to open fire, but he could see that at any moment he might lose sight of the terrorists. He decided to take a chance and told Jones to remain where he was and to open fire if he got a clear sight of the men whilst he worked his way back up the hill from where he could radio to Bessbrook for reinforcements and call forward his covering patrol. Leaving his radio operator to guide the covering patrol he then set off with Bourne to re-join Jones. At about 21.55 when they were still about 50 metres away from him Jones opened fire and almost immediately the terrorists shot back.

It was quite long range shooting, but Baughan and Bourne also opened up causing the four gunmen to separate; two took cover in a hedgerow and two in some old quarry workings near the house. Shots were still being traded and one terrorist was seen to run across an open field towards a gateway. The LMG fired at him and he was seen to drop onto his hands and knees crawling to a hedge which he managed to cross. Baughan saw that this man was still carrying his weapon as he made his way along a track where he disappeared from view. It was later learnt that this man was Patrick Malachy McParland of

*The Mountainhouse incident: the QRF taking a quick smoke after the incident (above), and Colour-Sergeant Baughan (second from right) with his patrol (below).*

*The author at the bungalow talking to a bearded RUC officer.*

Carrickananny (just two miles to the north) who was admitted to hospital in the Republic suffering from gunshot wounds the following day. He had been leader of the group.

Meanwhile my Gazelle had arrived overhead with Roger Miller onboard. He saw two terrorists make their way, unseen by Colour-Sergeant Baughan, to the bungalow and he directed the ARF, commanded by Simon Barry, to land near and tackle these two. This Simon did with considerable dash, some would say foolhardiness. He had only three men in addition to himself but he 'surrounded' the building and then attempted to converse with the gunmen to find out whether or not they were holding hostages. He smashed the front bedroom window with his rifle butt and called on them to surrender. They refused and a man in the house shouted that they would only surrender to the RUC. Despite a threat to throw a smoke grenade through the window the gunmen still refused to budge. However, two shots into the bedroom ceiling followed by a further two at the front porch had the desired effect and Patrick Joseph Quinn and Raymond Peter McCreesh both of Camlough came out unarmed. Inside the house Simon recovered an Armalite rifle, a Garand rifle and 270 live rounds. The two men were detained there in my presence and that of the parish priest until the RUC arrived to complete the arrest procedure.

Many more men had arrived on the scene by 22.30 and a search of the area quickly revealed a 9mm Sten gun lying on the track near to where the car had been seen originally, and the car itself which turned out to be a Peugeot estate car. We had captured only two men of the original five and I decided to stake out the area overnight using the B Company soldiers under Major Ian Chapman and carry out a more detailed search in the morning at about 05.00. Searching the bunkers where the men had first gone to ground they were astonished to find Daniel McGuinness of Camlough asleep with his Armalite cradled in his arms and 32 empty cartridge cases beside him. So the final tally was three captured and two escaped (one of whom had gunshot wounds). It could have been better but it could have been an awful lot worse.

Needless to say Saturday 26th June was a happy day. We were very pleased that at last we had achieved a success and it was a success that was well deserved and not a fluke. The original OP had been tasked to watch the Mountainhouse area because intelligence gleaned by a routine patrol had suggested that this area might be used for an ambush. We were not the only people to be pleased, for the brigade commander was in Bessbrook by 07.45 (shortening my night's sleep to just four hours) and to my delight CLF sent us a congratulatory message. Indeed goodwill messages came from all directions and there was a high degree of elation wherever one turned. I visited Forkill, Crossmaglen and the RUC Newry during the day to give them first hand accounts of what had occurred and a good day was rounded off by supper with the Chief Superintendent and his wife. I drove myself there again but on this occasion was more careful about my alcohol consumption. The last event of the day occurred at 22.00 when a RM rigid raider from HMS *Alert* was engaged with small arms fire by several weapons from the southern shore of Carlingford Lough. 36 rounds were fired back but no hits were claimed by either side.

The amount of positive publicity we achieved from this very successful action was virtually nil on either the Saturday or Sunday. It seemed that every time we had some sort of unfortunate nonsense we achieved hundreds of column inches immediately in the mainland and local press yet our occasional successes passed unremarked. The Mountainhouse Inn action was used by the NITAT team for years to come as a classic example of how to conduct an anti-terrorist action in Ulster, yet the Press were apparently unimpressed, and the Public Relations officers seemed powerless to convince them differently.

Sunday, 27th June, was a really quiet day and for the first time I remained in the Mill all day. In the evening we had organised a small party to say farewell to 661 Squadron AAC who had come to the end of their tour. We were sad to see them go, they had served us brilliantly and we were pleased that they were able to share our success, but our real concern at their departure was that we would have to start doing our own map-reading until the new squadron's pilots had learnt their way around.

The following day our brigade commander from Aldershot, Geoffrey Howlett, visited and I spent the whole day with him. It was a beautiful one, all the bases were immaculate, morale was excellent and the countryside looked appealing. He really could not have failed to be impressed. Once he had left, at 17.00 I went to the Musgrave Park Hospital to meet Mr and Mrs Snowdon. As I arrived, Mrs Snowdon had just finished telephoning her relatives to tell them that William had died earlier that afternoon. Naturally she was very distraught and it was a very difficult meeting. She was very brave and well supported by her husband, but the real tower of strength was a gem of a Red Cross girl called Lesley, who was quite superb with the Snowdons. I promised Mrs Snowdon that we would provide a bearer party, a bugler and some friends for the funeral and that David Cooper and I would also attend – it was the least we could do.

Life had to go on and I went straight from the Musgrave to a cocktail party at Ballykinler given by 1 QLR and afterwards to dinner with the CO, Malcolm Hinings. CLF was there and to my total surprise he was wearing an Airborne Forces tie – suddenly we had become popular. I was back at Bessbrook at 01.00 to spend an hour discussing intelligence matters with Pat Conn.

June ended with two extremely hot days and not much terrorist activity. Indeed, Tuesday 29th June was the hottest day ever recorded in Ulster and at long last we achieved a little publicity for the Mountainhouse action, albeit somewhat belatedly. We also managed to keep young Snowdon's death quiet as I judged that there was no point in giving the PIRA the satisfaction of knowing that he was dead.

The Army's Director of Combat Development, and incidentally a previous CO of 3 PARA visited at 11.00 for an hour. He and I had never really hit it off and this visit was to prove no exception. The routine at the entrance to the Mill was that all weapons had to be handed in to the guard commander. The General's escort, Sergeant Flowers of the RMP, handed over his pistol in a loaded condition and my guard commander, unfamiliar with the type of pistol, accidentally fired a shot whilst attempting to unload it. So as we walked down the corridor there was a muffled report which I hoped the General had not noticed – but of course he had. This accident set the tone for the visit perfectly.

# CHAPTER ELEVEN

# All Quiet

## *1st-19th July 1976*

July started very differently. We at Bessbrook had been
discussing taking some serious exercise, and in an effort to
tackle something quite challenging decided that we would go
for a hike in the Mourne Mountains (just above Newcastle,
County Down). None of us had any knowledge of the area but
we were aware of the annual Mourne Walk when thousands of
people follow the boundary wall around its circular course of
about twenty miles. The chosen group was the Battalion HQ
first XI: CO, Operations Officer, adjutant and padre,
accompanied by a number of willing volunteers (signallers and
clerks).

That first day of July was extremely hot and we wore few
clothes, and took very little with us except lunch, water and
some protection should the weather change dramatically. We
could see from the map that the line which the wall followed
was very up and down, but we were not really certain of how
difficult the route would prove. We had arranged that we
would be dropped by Wessex helicopter a little below Slieve
Donard, at 2,796 feet the highest point, and would then walk in
an anti-clockwise direction around the wall for about twelve
miles before heading off towards Rostrevor. We felt unable to
be certain about how far we would get in the time available so
we just gave the pilot a 'guesstimate' and told him that if we
were not at that place at 18.00 he should assume that we would
be further back down the route.

We set off in very good spirits and moving quite rapidly, but
it was quickly obvious that the Mournes are very steep and that
in particular going downhill was very hard on our out of
condition knees. The wall was a surprise, I had expected a

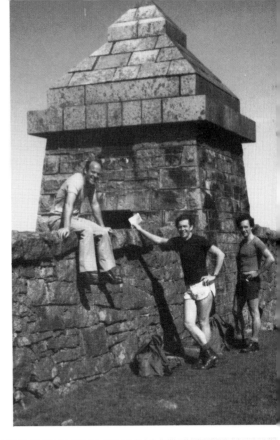

**Right** *The Mourne Wall. Left to right:*
*David Cooper, Andrew Dudzinski,*
*Richard Hoyle.*

**Below** *The Mourne Wall. Looking west*
*from Slieve Donard.*

normal dry stone wall of barely four feet, but this wall was something else, magnificently engineered, in perfect condition almost everywhere, and well over five feet high. The day was very very hot in the clear mountain air and the consequence was that our progress was not all that we might have hoped. How far we covered I cannot exactly recall, probably about eighteen miles, but I do remember only too vividly that each peak became more and more difficult to negotiate so that at about 16.30, as we virtually crawled up one not very steep hill on our hands and knees, having walked almost without stopping through the day, I called a halt. There was a great sigh of relief all round. Everyone in the party had had enough, but nobody had dared actually voice the thought. We gathered together in a small tight circle in the heather at the top to await the helicopter which was due at 18.00 and in no time at all we were sound asleep. The clatter of the low-flying Wessex, searching vainly for us wakened us with a start. Someone leapt to his feet, and attracted the helicopter pilot's attention and in a few moments a shattered, sunburnt, but very contented group climbed wearily aboard and promptly went to sleep again. It had been a day of spectacular views, comradeship, humour, and contact with the more healthy element in Ulster's population.

Nothing much had happened in our absence and that evening I watched our visiting 'Band Show'. This was a travelling circus organised by my bandmaster and consisting of my regimental band accompanied by a comedian and some strippers (paid for from our canteen profits) who had come over from England to entertain us. I was not very impressed by the comedian (who was rather too lewd for my taste) or the strippers (who were not all that exciting) but there was an excellent girl vocalist and the soldiers certainly thought the whole show was very worthwhile which was the object of the exercise. Over the next few days they entertained at each of the company bases that had sufficient space to accommodate them.

At the Brigade O Group on 2nd July Brigadier David was full of praise for our efforts the previous Friday and even gave me a glass of whisky (about the last thing I wanted at that time of day but it would have been churlish to refuse). I extracted myself and during the afternoon I visited Malcolm Cuthbertson at Forkill, the RUC in Newry, B Company and SAS Squadron in

*The Bandshow.*

Bessbrook. That evening several problems emerged which give a flavour of the background events which continued throughout the tour; a sergeant had an epileptic fit; I heard that a driver's wife was making free with her favours in Aldershot so I sent him back to sort it out; a soldier in B Company heard that his mother was extremely ill, so he was sent home on leave; Father Hughes and a doctor from Newtownhamilton visited to complain about our treatment of the Quinns (a family with strong PIRA connections); and the 180 page report on the Eglish affair was apparently distributed to everyone except us. The latter arrived the following day and told us nothing we did not already know. I wrote 'what an appalling waste of time and effort'. During the morning Brigadier David visited Forkill, Crossmaglen and Bessbrook and expressed his pleasure at the way in which we were improving each of the bases and later, after supper, I took my rover group out for a drive to Newry, Warrenpoint and Rostrevor. That evening was also the second consecutive Saturday on which we had run the Crossmaglen disco lure.

On Sunday evening I spent several hours with Pat and Roger (separately) in an effort to determine what was, and was not possible in terms of future initiatives. I was concerned that we might be running short of ideas but we discussed several, all of which seemed to have potential but none was too promising. The following day I did the rounds of the company bases and at tea time my new second-in-command and old friend, John Porter-Wright, arrived to begin taking over from Edward Gardener whom I was going to miss, for we made a good team.

At 18.30 I left Bessbrook by Gazelle to catch a flight to Heathrow. Surprisingly, with Newcastle barely 200 miles away in a straight line, the only way that I could be present at young Snowdon's funeral and be back in time for a Study Day at Lisburn which I had to attend at 10.00 on Wednesday, 7th July, was to fly via Heathrow. But as the early morning flight from Aldergrove would not allow me time to catch a train to Newcastle, and the return from Newcastle was too late to catch the last flight to Aldergrove, I finished up spending two brief nights at home. The funeral was due to start at 13.30 on Tuesday so my schedule was to catch the last shuttle to Heathrow, then drive home arriving at 23.00. Up again at

05.00 for the train journey to Newcastle, returning home again at 22.00. Then up again at 05.00 to Heathrow via Aldershot, catching the first shuttle which arrived just in time for the Study Day – 1400 miles by 'plane, train and car to complete 400. No wonder Ulstermen feel that public transport between them and England is poor and that they are somewhat isolated from the rest of the United Kingdom.

The funeral lasted an hour and was followed by a small low key wake. Poor Mrs Snowdon was very distressed but her husband supported her well and she lasted out bravely. I was glad that I had attended; these were lovely Geordies with an excellent tradition of service in the Army and they deserved every scrap of encouragement that we could give them. I left them in the capable hands of David Cooper who was travelling in slower time via the Stranraer ferry.

On my way through Aldershot on the Wednesday morning I was shown a copy of the battalion's daily report and learnt that the previous day two of my soldiers had been attacked in the Horseshoe Bar in Lisburn and had lost a pistol. I was horrified; I could not think what they had been doing in Lisburn, which was well outside our area, let alone what they were doing in the bar in civilian clothes. It transpired later that they had both attended the military dentist at Thiepval Barracks in Lisburn at 09.30 in the morning. Rather than tie up a car to wait for their treatment to be completed they were told that they would be collected at 15.30, and were given specific instructions by Sergeant Knox that they were not to leave the barracks. Dentistry over, and in flagrant disregard of this instruction they decided to walk into Lisburn and look round the shops. Lisburn is a staunch Protestant town so they assumed they would be safe from the attentions of terrorists, but they conveniently forgot the existence of the UVF, which is the Loyalist answer to PIRA.

Before leaving Bessbrook that morning they had each drawn up a service revolver with five rounds of ammunition, and these bulky items were difficult to conceal so they carried them in paper bags. At about 11.30 they decided to have a drink and they entered the Coachmans Public House where they drank two pints of beer each. They visited three further bars, consuming a pint of beer in each before returning to the

Coachmans where Private Hassell became involved in an argument with four girls and a man. One of the girls was questioning him about the contents of his paper bag and because of this they left the Coachmans and entered the Horseshoe Bar. Whilst in this bar Hassell (who by now was pretty drunk) dropped his paper bag on the floor and the revolver slid out. A man then entered the bar and offered to buy Hassell a drink and engaged him in a conversation about weapons and the Army. Hassell and he then visited the toilet, according to Hassell 'to try and gain some intelligence from the man'. They were in the toilet for some while and Lee entered it to find out what was happening. There he found Hassell and the man in heated argument. Just as he was about to leave the toilet Lee heard a scuffle behind him and then a bang and felt a pain in his right arm. The man ran into the bar carrying Hassell's pistol. According to Hassell the Irishman had grabbed his pistol and in an attempt to recover it there was a mêlée and a shot was fired. Hassell then grabbed Lee's pistol and chased after the man who instantly disappeared. Returning to the bar he asked for someone to telephone the RUC.

This discreditable performance caused a fully loaded pistol to fall into the hands of the Loyalist para-militaries, wounded one soldier (Lee) and humiliated 3 PARA. It was a perfect illustration of the suggestion in Chapter One that a battalion's good reputation is a very fragile thing.

One other significant incident occurred on 6th July during my absence. The battalion nightly report had simply mentioned:

> 08.30 hours explosion at grid reference 880139 on the Concession Road near Cullaville. Road now blocked by crater. Command wire ran south for over 200 metres. Milk churn fragments found, estimated at 300 lbs, command wire in place for some months. Possibly detonated by lightning.

and, my mind full of other things I gave it not a second thought. Only years later did I discover what actually happened. About ten days previously a patrol led by Sergeant Lucey of A Company had apprehended two men who were acting suspiciously but for reasons which nobody can recall he was ordered to release them. One of these men was subsequently killed by another unit. On 6th July Lucey was tasked to visit the area again as a civilian had reported seeing some suspicious wires. After questioning a farmer, Sergeant Lucey left eight of his men as a firm fire base while he took his remaining three men to search for the wires. They quickly found these partly hidden in a dry stone wall.

They were close to the border, in the narrow strip between the Concession Road and the River Fane (which is the border at this point) and Lucey was anxious to resolve the find quickly, so he attached a long line to the wires and pulled them from a distance to ensure that they were not booby trapped. All that happened was that more wire come out of the wall. Strictly speaking Lucey had already broken the rules and at this juncture he should certainly have radioed to his company HQ with a request for an ATO and an RE search team to come and clear whatever he had found. He decided against this, and instead connected one of his spare radio batteries to the wires. To his utter astonishment there was a devastating explosion on the Concession Road some 200-300 metres to the north of their position. Upon inspection a large crater was found which completely blocked this relatively busy road. Fortunately there were no civilian or military casualties.

Lucey had no option then but to inform his base because the explosion had been heard quite clearly at Crossmaglen two miles away and an ATO was tasked to examine the area to ensure that there were no further devices. Sergeant Lucey for his part could not admit to having initiated the explosion, hence the initial report of lightning. I know how he must have felt, I'd committed an almost identical error on my previous tour in South Armagh as it is always very tempting to 'do it yourself' in preference to summoning outside but expert assistance. Not surprisingly I was probably the last person in 3 PARA to learn the true story.

The Study Day was being run by the Army although much of it was concerned with the RUC and the audience was split between the two elements. I arrived just in time to hear the GOC's opening remarks which centred on some statistics and a great deal of praise for 3 PARA and the SAS. So much praise in fact that it was almost embarrassing, but it was the sort of embarrassment that I could put up with once in a while.

The remainder of the morning consisted of talks on the new position of the RUC (police primacy) and some ideas largely from the Chief Constable for the establishment of a crime squad. My Chief Superintendent and I voiced very strongly the need for much better forensic support than was currently available and during the final question session I asked the Secretary of State (Merlyn Rees) whether it would be possible to introduce an ID Card system in the Province. To my total amazement, for we had always understood that it was a 'political decision' not to introduce them, he replied 'if the GOC advises me that this would be helpful I would most certainly go ahead'. This was marvellous news but I was instantly deflated when the GOC said 'we'll discuss it afterwards' and then declined to.

The study ended with lunch and shortly afterwards I was able to slip away in time for my own weekly O Group where I was happy to pass on a number of nice messages from the GOC, and Brigadiers David Anderson and Geoffrey Howlett. Among other things that afternoon I asked the company commanders to be careful not to 'over-egg' our lures as I had the impression, rightly or wrongly, that PIRA could see through the traps we set for them far too easily. Subtlety was evidently absent.

Whilst I was at Lisburn two men armed with 9 mm automatics entered Fishers Timber Yard at Merchants Quay in Newry. They opened fire and hit a young man, Leslie Dodds, but their target was Jim Henning a part-time major in 3 UDR who escaped by jumping through a window. A classic illustration of the danger which is always present for any UDR soldier, especially when living or working in or near a predominantly Nationalist area.

Thursday, 8th July, was spent catching up on the paperwork but I also managed to complete a handful of citations for awards which I wanted to get David Anderson to support before he handed over. Nevertheless I still managed to visit all the bases and the RUC station and had a long chat with my new 2IC. Major John Porter-Wright and I, having attended Sandhurst together where we were in the same company, were old chums and I had no doubt that we would get on well again.

During the day Colin Thomson received the classic 'lure' message which everyone had been warned about during our training. The story went that at 01.30 in the morning four masked men had entered the public house at Creggan, a tiny village just a mile east of Crossmaglen. One man carrying a rifle had ordered the owners (Terence Grant and his wife) out and instructed them not to return until 02.30 nor to report the incident. Dutifully they did as they were told and returned much later (at 12.00) when they discovered a barrel with wires attached inside their pub. Colin's inclination was to get the ATO to deal with it but I put the brakes on hard. It was in just this sort of situation that I had lost two excellent SNCOs in 1973 and I was not going to be too helpful to the locals again, indeed I resolved that pub or no pub I would leave the situation untouched for as long as necessary. No one in the village seemed unduly worried at our inaction which was a help.

During the next two days I visited all the bases twice and hosted a farewell dinner to David Anderson which all of my company commanders attended together with the Chief Superintendent and HSB. It seemed very successful with the last guest (HSB) leaving at 02.30. Earlier in the day, in anticipation of the Brigadier's departure we had reoccupied Firebase Miller, the OP on the Dublin Road – we hoped that he would not notice. That Saturday, 10th July, was Airborne Forces Day in Aldershot and our wives attended in our stead.

The great Protestant marching day (12th July) passed peacefully in our area, largely I suspected because there were very few Protestants to cause trouble. Nevertheless, 7000 with 70 bands descended on Warrenpoint, a highly provocative activity which our good planning and the commonsense of the locals allowed to pass off in carnival atmosphere, helped by the marvellous weather. It was a case of ice creams all round – Protestants, Catholics, RUC and Army alike.

Patrolling very close to the border on 12th July between Forkill and Ballsmill Corporal Gardner of Patrol Company had found what he described over the radio as a 'bomb factory' in a derelict building. He was instructed to ambush the site although his patrol's presence must have been noticed as their find had been made in daylight. The following morning a group of children were sent by the PIRA to the area to check

*Warrenpoint, 12 July 1976.*

whether the patrol was still there. Having been discovered, Corporal Gardner decided to withdraw but when they did they were fired at from just across the border. A full follow up was organised and the 'bomb factory' cleared. It consisted of 120 lbs of home made explosive plus some commercial explosive, a timing device and an auto handling device. None of these were armed and the kit was clearly being stored prior to use elsewhere. It was a good find in a very unfavourable area.

In the evening HMS *Vigilant* (*Alert*'s sister ship) was just slipping from the dock at Warrenpoint when it came under automatic fire from the opposite side of the river, that is from the Republic. Between 100 and 200 rounds were fired, none of which hit the vessel, some however landed in the Hurricane Cafe on the Dockside, slightly injuring one civilian. In the immediate response *Vigilant* fired 110 rounds into the Republic but no hits were claimed, and the Garda and Irish Army in following up arrested no one.

These two incidents illustrated all too clearly how the safe haven of the Republic was being used by the terrorists. In neither case had the terrorists crossed into Northern Ireland and in both their shots crossed an international boundary. Imagine my irritation therefore when the following day all the Irish newspapers carried the headline story that we had crossed the border to arrest the culprits.

However, serious incidents were becoming rarer in South Armagh, so much so that when CLF visited us in the afternoon of Thursday 15th July he wanted to know why the area was so quiet. I knew why the area was quiet – we were working hard and effectively and I told him so, to which he retorted that it was 'always quiet in the summer and that he expected terrorist activity to be stepped up in August' (when we had departed). His forecast was to prove accurate but solely, in my view, because we had the PIRA guessing (a view which was later confirmed by other sources).

Friday, 16th July, was David Anderson's last day in command of 3 Infantry Brigade and champagne followed his O Group, after which I discussed the Creggan public house bomb with the Civil Affairs Adviser at Brigade HQ and we decided there and then to burn the pub down in preference to disarming the bombs. Later I did the round of my bases and then settled down in the evening to write to General Sir Frank King, then Commander of NATO's Northern Army Group and Commander-in-Chief of BAOR on the role of 3 PARA during their coming three years in Germany. General Frank had been my CO way back in 1960 (I had been his IO) and it was good to think of something away from South Armagh and the Irish.

On Sunday 17th July, just after midnight, a number of mortar bombs were fired at Support Company's base in Newry. There were no hits, and the only damage was to adjacent civilian property. As the base was situated in a very residential area it is easy to appreciate quite how irresponsible the attack was. The local PIRA unit said 'seven mortars hit the post. After the attack part of the Centre was ablaze. The British have not admitted the damage caused to the Centre or their casualties'. This was another example of the lies of the PIRA propagandists.

Our leisure time, such as it was, had taken a dramatic upturn that week for the Olympic Games had started in Montreal. The excellent and continuous television coverage meant that watching the 'box' could become a bit more meaningful for a fortnight. However, patrolling was kept up at the same unrelenting pace and during the day two speculative searches (in this case of walls and trees) turned up ammunition finds of over 350 rounds, one on the border near H25, and the other in Newry.

*The Times* of 19th July carried an excellent article by Henry Stanhope, the Defence Correspondent, entitled 'The Army digs in for a long stay as Ulster realises there are no easy solutions'. It was a perceptive article and it was most encouraging to realise that the responsible press was at last getting the message that the Ulster problem was not going to be resolved quickly.

# CHAPTER TWELVE

# The Last Lap

## *20th July – 8th August 1976*

We were left with exactly four weeks although I cannot recall registering the fact at the time. However, I do recall wondering what that last period would bring – further success, boredom, or disaster. Had we been superstitious we would have been nervous, for the first event occurred at 06.55 at Bessbrook Mill. Two bored soldiers on sentry were fiddling with a revolver and in the process Private Evans received a gunshot wound to his stomach. The accident was largely his fault and he of all people had no excuse as he was a first class shot and as a member of the battalion shooting team he had recently returned from competing at Bisley.

At lunchtime the GOC visited and spent some time talking to the SAS troopers and to Patrol Company soldiers before flying to Crossmaglen where A Company was being commanded by Captain Donald Cuthertson-Smith during Colin's absence on R & R. At 16.00 Mr Brian Cubbon, the Permanent Under Secretary to the Northern Ireland Office, arrived for a briefing before making his way to Dublin where he was to meet and stay with the new British Ambassador. That evening eight high velocity rounds were fired from across the border at Firebase Miller, 135 rounds were returned at long range and no hits were claimed. However, the Garda apprehended five men and carted them off to Dundalk for questioning. Our prediction for Firebase Miller was beginning to prove correct.

That evening also we were visited by Lieutenant Colonel Brian Campbell who, as CO of the Royal Highland Fusiliers (1 RHF), was due to succeed 40 Commando RM in Bessbrook before Christmas. He was on his initial visit to the area and it certainly brought it home to us that we were nearing the end of our own tour.

Wednesday, 21st July, brought the tragic news from Dublin that the Ambassador's car had been blown up by the PIRA. The Ambassador (who had visited us exactly four weeks previously) and his secretary, Judy Cooke, were killed. Brian Cubbon was seriously injured but thankfully made a full recovery.

The day, however, brought one happy event when we were visited by General Sir Roland Gibbs, Chief of the General Staff (the Army's premier appointment). It was almost his first full day in his new post and I, as custodian of his old battalion, was delighted that we were so honoured. It was nearly but not quite a perfect visit. In March when he had visited us during our training in Kent most of the lunch had already been consumed and he wrote in thank you '... for a marvellous lunch – it was a pity they had eaten all the peas the day before!'. On this occasion I cannot recall what happened but I wrote in my diary 'Good visit apart from an appalling lunch', but he either did not notice, or more likely was much too polite to mention it for he wrote to me the following day in his own hand, thanking me 'for a very good lunch'.

At 14.10 we set fire to the Creggan Inn. It was a lovely blaze and completely gutted the main part of the building. Nearly two weeks had elapsed since the problem had first been reported to us and although the owners had from time to time asked us to get on with making their inn safe, no one else exerted any pressure at all – for the PIRA in South Armagh patience was the watchword. To tackle such a situation by burning was unusual, probably unique. My decision had the support of the GOC and Chief Constable but most reassuring was the result. The building contained three devices, two were destroyed in the fire and the other, of about 10 lbs of explosive, was subsequently disarmed. Almost certainly, had ATO been tasked to clear the building using the well established procedures, one or more devices would have been triggered and his death would have been the result. This way, there was no loss of life and heavy compensation was averted when we proved that most of the bottles and barrels had in fact been empty.

Admiral Sir Anthony Troup, RN Flag Officer Scotland and Northern Ireland, visited the following day, ostensibly to look at HMS *Vigilant* on Carlingford Lough. Meanwhile I went round Crossmaglen and Forkill, and later to RUC Newry. My nightly call to Paddy that night was a bit distressing. She had returned from the Wives Club at about 23.00 but she was pretty frustrated that fewer than she had hoped had attended and some of the wives who did were becoming a bit tetchy. Whereas the soldiers could not tell me what they thought of me, the wives had no such inhibitions with Paddy. I felt very sorry for her, she was doing her duty as a good loyal Army wife and many of the remarks directed towards her were very unkind and uncalled for. Some wives tended to blame her quite unreasonably for their husband's absence.

Brigadier David Woodford's first O Group on Friday, 23rd July, turned out to much the same as his predecessor's. After it I was made aware of a new and strange occurrence which Support Company was accused of perpetrating. It seemed that on Saturday, 17th July, during the afternoon Michael, the fourteen-year-old son of Eileesh Morley, wife of the self-proclaimed 'Commanding Officer of the Provisionals' Prisoners of War, Long Kesh' was playing with a transister radio in the garden of their council house on the Derrybeg Estate, Newry. Fiddling about with the tuning he was suddenly astonished to pick up his mother's voice, and a subsequent search of the house revealed a listening device which was subsequently displayed at a press conference held on the 23rd. The accusation was that the 'bug' must have been planted by Support Company during a routine search of the house on 11th June.

Knowing the emotion that normally surrounds all suggestions of eavesdropping in mainland Britain (telephone tapping, industrial espionage, 'bugging' etc) I was fearful that the Republican publicity machine would again get some unfair cover at the expense of 3 PARA. In the event, however, the coverage was very light, most reporters seeming to peddle the line that 'this is an anti-terrorist campaign and we would expect the security forces to use every means to obtain information.'

During the afternoon there were two occurrences in the Forkill area which were classics, just the sort of situations for which everyone had been alerted during the preparatory training. The first occurred at 17.24 when Philip Nolan of Crossmaglen drove a blue Vauxhall Viva into Forkill village and parked it about 40 metres from the front entrance of the base. He gave a warning that there was a time bomb in the car and the area was cleared. His story was that he had been stopped just south of the border and been ordered out of his car by a masked man armed with a rifle. A few minutes later he was ordered back into the car, told there was a time bomb in the boot with an hour to run, and to deliver the car to the Forkill base. This was what we called a 'proxy bomb' and it demanded quick thinking if unnecessary damage was to be averted. The best possible action was for a brave volunteer to leap into the car and drive it away or to order the driver to drive it away. However, in this case that was not done; indeed there was a very long and inexcusable delay because the sangar sentry could not raise the company operations room on his intercom which was faulty, and could not attract the attention of anyone else. So there was the ridiculous situation in which a car bomb was just down the road with the driver standing unprotected at the front gate (needless to say none of this came to light at the time). The car had to be tackled and this was attempted by firing a Carl Gustav anti-tank practice rocket at the boot of the car to open it up and disrupt the wiring of any bomb inside, and then followed up by the ATO with Wheelbarrow (the robot). On this occasion it was quickly established that the boot was empty which seemed odd but at about the same time it was drawn to our attention that a tractor and trailer, which had previously been reported stolen, had reappeared and were at that moment parked a further 100 metres away. When stolen the trailer was empty, but now it contained a full load of straw which was very suspicious indeed not least as it was midsummer (this time it was PIRA who were lacking sophistication). Using a small incendiary grenade the straw was quickly ignited and when the goodly blaze had died away a gas cylinder became visible in the ashes.

The following day, after it had all cooled down it was established that the gas cylinder had contained about 30 lbs of home made explosive and was designed to be triggered by radio control. The probable plot had therefore been that the car should be parked by the front gate of the base, instead of 40 metres away. The only place from which the gate could be seen clearly was beside the farm trailer so that the hope was that the

*The Forkill proxy bomb: hosing down the haycart (above), and the haycart showing the cylinder (below).*

ATO could be blown up as he made his preparations to deal with the car. An excellent plan failed partly through the alertness of the soldiers and civilians, partly through the failure of the car driver to park at the correct spot, partly because it was all a bit too obvious, and partly because it was clearly our lucky day.

The second Forkill incident that day concerned a clip of 8 Garand rifle rounds which had been seen lying on the ground some time previously. Only the PIRA used Garands so the temptation was to pick up the rounds, but in this case the patrol finding them reacted absolutely correctly by doing nothing except to report the find as a suspected IED. ATO dealt with the rounds which were connected, as suspected, to a booby trap device of another gas cylinder containing 25 lbs of home-made explosive plus an assortment of scrap iron. So in the space of a day two very nasty traps had been avoided by the Forkill company, for had any soldier attempted to pick up the rounds they would have been blown to smithereens.

There had been very little 'cowboy' shooting by PIRA during our tour but on Saturday, 24th July, things, suddenly changed. At 09.50 two weapons (an M1 carbine and an Armalite) were fired at the front gate sentry of the Newry base. Eight shots were returned but no hits were claimed and it seemed that the terrorists had escaped by car into a neighbouring council estate. Then at 14.20 one low velocity round was fired at a Support Company patrol in the market area of Newry, the shot missed its target and instead lodged in the arm of a lady who was out shopping. She was taken to hospital where she fortunately made a quick recovery. At 18.35 the medical officer's vehicle was shot at by two youths armed with air rifles, again in Newry, and later at 21.37 three high velocity shots were fired at long range at a B Company patrol a few miles NW of Newry. What had brought on this spate of bravado was unclear but I allowed myself the mischievously cynical thought that perhaps PIRA was taking a cue from the appearance of our new brigade commander, who much to my amazement on his first visit to the battalion had worn a pair of brown cowboy boots with zip fasteners. My soldiers were certainly not impressed. More seriously though, it could have been a spontaneous response to the news of the Eileesh Morley bug which was given good coverage in the Irish newspapers that morning. PIRA always liked to react positively when they had suffered a set-back and they would have seen the Morley affair as a set back for themselves as well as an opportunity to turn it to their advantage to gain some publicity at our expense.

Early the following morning incendiary devices were ignited in two shops in Newry, completely gutting them, and then all went quiet for several days. This was fortunate for the Olympic Games were reaching a climax and it gave us every opportunity to keep abreast of the action. There was also plenty to do. With three weeks to go my O Group on 27th July was an ideal moment to try to ensure that we did not fall into the trap of dropping our guard as the end of the tour loomed nearer. We were also in for some personality changes, Edward Gardener and Andrew Dudzinski were due to leave us at the end of the week and the officer in charge of the RM detachment, Leo Williams, was going too. I stressed at the O Group that we must keep up the overt and covert patrolling pressure to the end, be particularly careful to check search any civilians entering a base, expect each base to be attacked before mid August, and start spring cleaning everywhere so that we hand over to 40 Commando RM in immaculate order. Finally I gave them a timely warning for the Anniversary of Internment which would be celebrated by the Republicans over the period 8th-10th August.

That evening although there were still three days to go before they left, we officially said farewell to Edward Gardener and Andrew Dudzinski who between them produced rather a lot of beer and wine. The party got a little out of hand and we certainly consumed more than our daily quota of alcohol.

The following morning the new brigade commander visited every base and then took lunch with us at Bessbrook. He had clearly been impressed and delighted by our standards for he was bubbling with enthusiasm and offered no shred of criticism or advice. This was confirmed later by his deputy and by H. Jones, both of whom telephoned to let me know that we had scored a first round win. It was an encouraging start in our relationship with Brigadier David Woodford.

I had been concerned that our move out of South Armagh on 17th August was due to follow a familiar pattern and could be an easy prey to a PIRA ambush. The normal routine was that everyone would be taken by helicopter to Bessbrook and thence by road to Belfast docks. The first part of the road journey out of Bessbrook was entirely predictable as there were only two routes between the main road running north from Newry and Bessbrook. Both ran through strong Republican areas and I decided that we could eliminate most of the risk by avoiding these two routes and instead helicoptering direct to a site somewhere on the main road, so in the afternoon I went out in my car to find a suitable field. I was very content with my choice and felt very much more relaxed about the move out, so much so that in the evening I confirmed with Paddy that we would take a house in the Isle of Wight for a fortnight on my return, a decision which I had been putting off for some weeks.

At 02.00 on 29th July I was woken to be told that an RUC constable had been shot dead at the Bessbrook village check point (just outside the front gate of the Mill and manned by 3 PARA). My immediate reaction was to fear the worst – that a sentry had had a negligent discharge but the reality was somewhat different. Just after 01.40 a car had approached the barrier at some speed and Private Craise, who was on duty there with Private Jackson, lay his rifle down on the floor of the sangar and stood in front of the barrier waving his torch. The approaching car stopped sharply just two feet from Craise who went to the driver's door where he shone his torch into the driver's face.

He did not recognise the man, and commenting on his erratic driving he requested to see his driving licence. The driver refused to produce it and Craise realised by his demeanour that he had been drinking. When the driver refused a second time Craise threatened to arrest him and told Jackson to notify the Guardroom that he was about to arrest two men. One of the men then said they were RUC constables but not seeing any uniform Craise again asked to see a driving licence or some other means of identity. Craise was becoming angry and Jackson anticipating a nasty scene, came out of the sangar and stood a short distance behind Craise from where he could see the driver more clearly. Craise again said he was going to arrest the men and turned his back on them to walk to the sangar to summon assistance.

As he did so, Jackson saw the driver reach into his pocket and produce something in his right hand which looked like a weapon. He cocked his rifle to the ready position and the driver stretched his arm out of the window and Jackson saw clearly that he had a pistol which he was pointing at Craise's retreating back. Believing the man was about to shoot Craise he shouted a warning and fired one shot. The driver slumped forward over the steering wheel and was certified dead by Alistair MacMillan (the doctor) a few minutes later.

It transpired that the driver was Reserve RUC Constable George Johnson. He and his companion, another Constable, had left their duty station in Newry much earlier than the proper end of their shift. Prior to leaving the RUC station they had drunk several pints of beer each and they then drank more in Norman Brown's public house in Newry. They were just about to leave the pub when they met two very young girls whom they already knew. They stayed talking to them until 00.30 when at the invitation of the youngest they drove to her house where her mother made tea for them. An hour later at 01.30 all four left in his car for Johnson's flat in Bessbrook and it was at the Bessbrook barrier that their escapade came to its dramatic and sad end. Luckily the two girls and the other passenger were uninjured.

My feelings about the incident were somewhat mixed. Naturally I was very sorry that one of my soldiers had killed the Constable and I was especially concerned for the dead man's wife and family. On the other-hand I could only conclude that Johnson behaved very irresponsibly and reaped an entirely predictable consequence. Certainly no blame could attach to Jackson who took immediate and effective action to protect his colleague.

Nevertheless I felt sufficiently moved to attend the funeral at Rathfriland two days later. It was a curious affair, Presbyterian, with no church service, just a short service at his home followed by a rather morbid procession around the village. All in all a very sombre conclusion to a most unnecessary event.

Less than an hour after Johnson's death a van containing an estimated 200 lbs of home made explosive detonated in Monagham Street, Newry, causing extensive damage. Fortunately PIRA had telephoned a warning and the area had

*Bessbrook village checkpoint.*

been cleared in sufficient time to avoid any casualties. Then at 02.35, 03.01 and 03.25 there were reports of shots in the Bessbrook village area but we took these with a pinch of salt, our sentries were probably hearing the local crowscarer.

Finally on Friday 30th July I said farewell to Edward and Andrew. I was genuinely very sorry to see them go. We had been a very happy team and whilst I had no doubt that we would survive without them there was bound to be an uneasy period as the confidence of the new team in each other became established. A few days later, Edward in a letter was kind enough to say; 'I have now completed over eight years with 3 PARA and served under some fairly distinguished Commanding Officers. In all that time I have never known the battalion to be in better shape than it is now.'

Once they had departed I went out to Crossmaglen to go on patrol with Sergeant Sergeant. He was an old friend, having been a private soldier in A Company when I was commanding it some years previously in Malta. He was a very good soldier, keen, thorough and professional. I was most impressed by the patrol and concluded that they were unlikely to get shot at and would never do anything silly.

In the evening the Bessbrook sentry's jitters continued when they reported that a dark-coloured car had at 22.55 appeared fleetingly some distance from the Bessbrook village barrier and the rear seat passenger had fired two low velocity shots at the sentry post. This was not imagination though, as it was confirmed by a passing civilian. Again the following morning in the early hours shots were heard in Bessbrook but this was the last report of such 'noises off' and we reverted to our normal peaceful existence. It may well be that the noises heard were of someone testing a pistol for at 01.50 Eugene McCullough was walking home when he was approached by some men who shot him twice in each leg. We never found out who was responsible.

When I woke on Saturday, 31st July I was informed that there had been an explosion at Crossmaglen at 06.12. What had apparently happened was that Sergeant Sergeant's patrol was returning into the Crossmaglen base. As they arrived at the front gate they noticed an Army issue torch lying on the ground. Sergeant had arranged his men to give him protection from surprise whilst he himself went up to the torch and using his hook and line (which all NCOs carried) pulled the torch. It moved six or seven feet towards the main gate when it became caught in a wire mat and exploded, much to his amazement. Four men were injured slightly (temporary deafness), but enough to warrant their removal to hospital for observation. On later examination it seemed that the booby-trapped torch had been packed with four ounces of commercial explosive – enough to cause a death or two. Sergeant was very unwise to have taken the action that he did, but he would have been even more stupid to have picked the torch up. Nevertheless I was moved to visit Crossmaglen shortly afterwards to ensure that he learnt directly from me just how silly I thought he had been. He was naturally rather contrite but it did not dampen his effervescent spirit.

The first two days of August were totally quiet but on the third Captain Tombs, a UDR officer, was nearly assassinated in Bridge Street, Newry and in the follow up we were also lucky to avoid injury. What happened was that at 09.30 Captain Tombs was travelling to work in his car when at a junction he came under fire from quite close range. Six Armalite rounds were fired from behind a garden wall and Tombs received three bullet fragments in his chest which necessitated his evacuation to hospital. It transpired that four terrorists had hi-jacked the getaway car some hours previously and had kept the owner, John Hillen, hooded in a house for four hours whilst the ambush took place. The terrorists had booby-trapped their firing point and only an observant soldier seeing a piece of fishing line stretched across a path prevented someone walking into the explosive force of three pounds of home made explosive packed with masonry nails.

CLF visited at 12.30 to make his farewell calls to all of the companies. It seemed a little premature, but for some good reason which I cannot recall now the visit had had to be arranged then. He seemed in very good form and appeared to enjoy himself hugely. Nevertheless he was still obsessed with the thought that incidents occur more frequently in South Armagh in the winter than they do in the summer, which I know now for a fact is quite unsubstantiated.

I was beginning to feel bored for the first time since the tour began, and even my O Group on Wednesday, 4th August, dealing as it did with our plans for the Anniversary of Internment; the knowledge that the PIRA had three Armalites in Newry; making arrangements for the Advance Party to move back to Aldershot; talking to the company commanders about reorganising the battalion after the tour and our impending posting to BAOR did nothing to dispel the mood. Indeed I even borrowed a tape recorder that evening to re-start my German language course.

Thursday, 5th August was another quiet day. I visited all the bases, as I had now done on just about every day during the tour, and the RUC station. I also flew in to Firebase Miller, now re-christened Phoenix (having arisen from the ashes of its predecessor), where I noted that it sported a provocative, but nevertheless apposite, Union Jack.

The cowboy shooting resumed on that day with shots fired at our permanent VCP on the O'Meath road and the following day a determined attack was launched on the front of the Newry base when 30-40 Armalite rounds were fired with, uncharacteristically, the firing continuing for a brief period after the sentries had fired sixteen rounds back towards their attackers. The same afternoon the RUC station at Warrenpoint was lucky to avoid serious damage when a car parked alongside it and containing 100 lbs of home-made explosive failed to detonate correctly. Only two windows were broken.

A classic illustration of the pitfalls connected with intelligence and human sources arose early on Saturday, 7th August. I was woken up at 05.00 by a very excited Joe Baker, accompanied by his IO. Apparently someone had walked into their Newry base with some really good information. I should have known better, but I agreed to let them search seven occupied houses which they did at 06.35. In terms of organisation it was a miracle, for in that one and a half hours not only were the soldiers briefed but RE search teams were organised and WRAC girls flown down from Portadown. But the result was to find two shotguns and to incur the wrath of HSB, because we had not cleared the searches with him. One will never know, but in all probability at least one of the houses searched belonged to one of his contacts. Certainly the result was a distinct frostiness, and he failed to attend the SAS Squadron's farewell drinks party that evening although everyone else came including the brigade commander and his staff.

Sunday, 8th August, was a beautiful day, at least to begin with. It was very sunny, the sort of day when one was pleased to be alive. I visited all the bases and the RUC Station, my boredom lifted and I was very content. At about 16.15 Private John Borucki was part of an unscheduled patrol returning into the Crossmaglen base. Corporal McKinley, the patrol commander, was leading with Borucki following a little behind him as he turned from the Crossmaglen Market Square into the Cullaville Road, just 100 metres from the front entrance to the base. The other five members of the patrol were following Borucki at intervals.

As McKinley turned the corner, he noticed an old fashioned black bicycle leaning against the wall of the building on his side of the road. On the rear carrier of the cycle he saw a parcel wrapped in blue material, but the bicycle did not arouse his suspicion as he recognised it as one belonging to an old man who lived in the village. He continued on past it and stopped to look into the rear of a van parked on the pavement in front of him. As he did so he noticed that Borucki had rounded the corner and was standing alertly near the bicycle. As he returned his attention to the van he was suddenly aware of an explosion which flung him to the ground. Picking himself up he first thought that the explosion had occurred at the opposite side of the street, but on walking back towards the corner he saw the body of Borucki lying in the middle of the road. The air was thick with the acrid black smoke caused by the explosion but as it cleared he noticed the remains of the bicycle which were also scattered around the area. He immediately summoned assistance from the base but Borucki, sadly, was beyond medical aid as he had taken the full force of what was later estimated to be about 5 lbs of commercial explosive triggered by radio control. Fortunately no one else was injured.

It was one of those things that we knew could happen at any time. No blame could be attached to anyone; it was child's play for PIRA to set up a device in a vehicle or even a pram and trigger it by radio control as they did in this case. In a reasonably busy market town one could not possibly treat everything as suspicious and the only surprise was that the terrorists did not feel moved to attempt it more often. Leaving Richard Hoyle my adjutant to arrange for someone in England to break the news to the parents, I flew to Crossmaglen to get a full story and see how people were reacting. Then back to Bessbrook to phone Paddy so that she had an accurate picture and to learn that Richard had managed to fix for Captain Bill Bell, our Aldershot rear party officer, who happened to be at his home only some 30 miles from Worksop, where the Boruckis lived, to visit and give them the tragic news. That done I returned to Crossmaglen where I found everyone reacting splendidly and philosophically except Colin who took the killing very personally, although he had no reason at all to reproach himself.

It was already clear that I would not be able to attend the funeral at such an important time in our tour but I arranged for suitable representation led by Colin and David Cooper, the padre. I decided that I would try and see the parents on the day that we got back to England.

This sad Sunday closed with one lighthearted moment. Two armoured vehicles belonging to 2 RRF, which were attached to Support Company for the weekend, accidentally drove 100

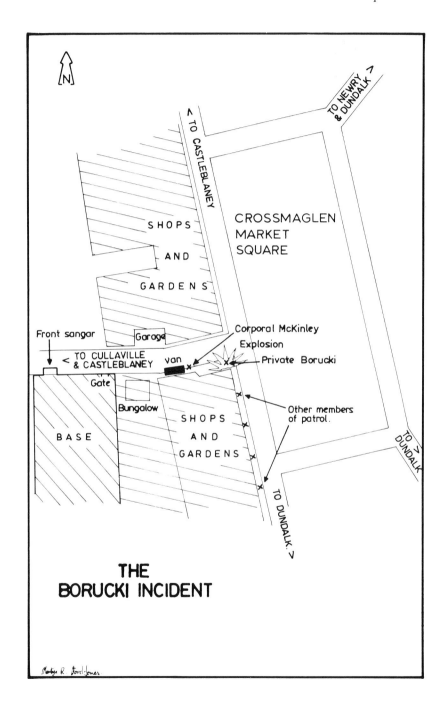

THE
BORUCKI INCIDENT

*Crossmaglen base (centre) and the point where Borucki was murdered (extreme right centre).*

metres into the Republic on the main Dublin Road before being turned back by the Garda. This aroused no comment at all – a sure sign that border incursions had resumed their previous level of unimportance. Indeed I noted in my diary that the Garda had been particularly helpful all day. In Ulster one could always find a silver lining to every black cloud.

# CHAPTER THIRTEEN

# Tragedy

## *9th-18th August 1976*

Traditionally the Republicans celebrate (commemorate is probably a more apposite word) the anniversary of internment by getting up very early and making one hell of a racket. 1976 was the fifth anniversary, and what they are remembering is 9th August 1971 when the Army arrested nearly 350 suspects who were then imprisoned without trial principally at Long Kesh, a disused wartime airfield. What happened was that the Army pounced at dawn and those who were first awakened banged dustbin lids and anything else which would make a suitable noise to warn their neighbours that the round up was in progress. The anniversary, therefore, traditionally starts with the noise at about 04.00 followed by other acts of disorder such as hi-jacking, rioting, erection of barricades and the like.

Much of the impact of the anniversary can be reduced by a heavy RUC and Army presence on the streets during the relevant period and our joint planning had gone ahead to achieve a peaceful day. I did not wake up to hear the natives beating their tom toms but rose at my normal time (07.00) to hear that everything was proceeding smoothly. There were throughout the day seventeen bomb hoaxes, all of which were rapidly dealt with, and a small peaceful march of about 350 people. It was the quietest anniversary that Newry had experienced and the RUC Superintendent was ecstatic. I went out with my rover group on three occasions during the day specifically looking for trouble but there was none to be found.

Imagine my fury, therefore, when the Ulster news at lunchtime announced that 'there had been a lot of hi-jacking in Newry'. I was livid and was on to the HQNI Press Desk immediately. Total fabrication of events by mediamen who do not bother to get off their backsides to find out what is really happening is at least half of the Ulster problem. There is nothing more galling than to be celebrating the success of your efforts at a time when the rest of the country, through the pernicious media, think that chaos reigns. At the District Action Committee meeting that week the Superintendent stated that 'the quietness in Newry over the anniversary was indicative of the tight control both by Support Company in Newry and the remainder of 3 PARA in general over South Armagh'. I could not disagree.

On Tuesday evening I had all the SAS squadron officers together with four from 2 RRF to the mess for a farewell drink. The SAS squadron was due to change over the following day, the day on which Julian Thompson would arrive with his advance party. D Squadron had done very well, they had worked very hard indeed and had not let the saga of the border incursion put them off their stroke. They had no notable success but had laid the foundations by sheer application for those who were to follow. They had amassed a huge quantity of information and had earned the respect and trust of the RUC, HQNI and ourselves. They had completely erased the idea (often voiced by the ignorant and the PIRA) that the SAS were in the 'dirty tricks' business. Better ambassadors for 22 SAS could not have been found.

Whilst we were having our farewell drinks, Phoenix was again showing its value. A foot patrol returning to the OP was fired at, the three high velocity rounds causing no damage. But the Phoenix gunner immediately returned the fire and 66 rounds of machine gun ammunition was probably more than the terrorists had bargained for. The Garda set up a road block to try to catch the culprits and even gave permission for us to fly over the border with our Nitesun (a powerful helicopter mounted searchlight).

Subconsciously we had waited for 11th August for nearly four months for that was the day that 40 Commando RM began to arrive in some strength. Their advance party was late and I was struck by the huge number of extraneous boxes and suitcases which they seemed to have with them. They clearly travelled with more kit than we did in 3 PARA. However, they were eventually farmed out to the relevant bases and I took

Julian to see Phoenix so that he could decide whether he was going to retain it or whether we should dismantle it before we departed.

I was obviously getting a bit restless for I decided that I would take my rover group on a drive round my old 1973 haunts. Strictly speaking military vehicles were totally banned in the area that we would visit but because we had stopped driving there so PIRA had stopped laying landmines; in consequence there was no danger whatsoever. We went therefore after dark to Forkill, Mullagabane, Silverbridge, Creggan, Crossmaglen, Cullyhanna, Belleek and Camlough. It was pleasant for me to see it all again from road level and for my crew it was a great adventure into no man's land. On our return I enjoyed a quick celebratory nightcap with the doctor, as it was his wedding anniversary.

On 12th August we ran a large convoy into Forkill and I visited the RUC station twice during the day. The following morning we were to assist the RUC to arrest five suspected terrorists which was rather more than the usual quota of one or two each day, and I wanted to be certain that we were properly coordinated. In the evening Joe Baker was holding a farewell party in Newry, principally for the RUC, and I went along for good measure. It went well, but the Ulstermen seemed rather chauvinistic for unfortunately we had all the men in one corner and the women in the other.

If one is at all superstitious, Friday the 13th has an uneasy feel about it, especially in an environment like Ulster where mistakes and mishaps occur readily no matter the date or day of the week. For us however, it was a normal day. The lift of the five men was successful though not altogether smooth and later in the day I was pleased to learn from the HSB that at least one had made an admission. Julian Thompson accompanied me later to my last Brigade O Group which was a very routine affair but it allowed him the opportunity to meet all the other commanding officers in the brigade.

At 10.15 the following morning an Ulster bus was hi-jacked in Newry and it shortly appeared under the eyes of one of our covert OPs where it got stuck across the road and two men were seen to run away. An Ulster bus driver was despatched to recover it but he found on arrival that it had a milk churn inside so our ATO was sent later to deal with it. Treating the bus as an IED he set fire to it. On examination later the churn turned out to be an expensive hoax or more likely a lure which went wrong through bad driving.

Routine familiarisation patrolling was by now well under way. All the overt patrols out at this time included members of 40 Commando RM and the SAS learning their way around. So instead of well coordinated patrols the members of which were used to each other, we had something of a hotchpotch. One of these patrols was to go tragically wrong.

That Saturday morning I was briefing Clare Hollingworth (*Daily Telegraph* Defence Correspondent) on South Armagh's problems and she was accompanied by Brigadier David. The briefing over, a pleasant morning was interrupted by the news that there had been a shooting near Whitecross and in the 'crossfire' between terrorists and a B Company patrol, a young girl had been shot and seriously injured. We finished our pre-lunch drink by which time the story had changed somewhat. The girl was dead and the story of the 'crossfire' was a little less certain. We started our lunch, but halfway through a further message caused me to excuse myself and go straight out to the scene.

When I arrived there it was far from clear why we were getting such a confused story, but slowly we got nearer to the facts. The confusion of course was reflected in the news bulletins and the story being put out by the Press Desk at HQNI, but they all stemmed from the fact that the only soldier who really knew what happened, the patrol's General Purpose Machine Gun (GPMG) gunner, was shocked and frightened because a child had been killed. The one uncontrovertible fact was that this unfortunate Private was one of my men and no matter what my own personal opinion of events might be as the story unfolded I intended to back him to the hilt as he would, quite inevitably, face prosecution for his action on that morning. He had been doing his best, and had he hit a gunman rather than a young girl we would have been ecstatic.

The principal problem in unravelling what happened was that the evidence of the patrol members, five of whom were from B Company 3 PARA and six were Marines from 40 Commando RM, conflicted. The object of the patrol had been to familiarise the Marines with the region and to meet some of the local people in this mixed area where Catholics and Protestants lived contentedly side by side. To this end the patrol commander, Second Lieutenant Nick Kirk, stopped at the entrance to the Ballymoyer cemetery so that he could introduce Seamus Reavey, who was tending a grave there with three other people, to the Marines. While this was going on, the patrol split into two groups with four men under Lance-Corporal Burton moving just a little down the road to the east where they set up a VCP. To protect this VCP Burton sent his GPMG gunner and two others a further 50 metres to the east. The road was undulating and the GPMG was facing downhill looking eastwards and in particular toward the hedges surrounding St Malachy's RC Church some 200 metres away.

All three groups, those by the churchyard, at the VCP and with the GPMG remembered a group of young girls and boys moving happily down the road towards the church and some of the soldiers exchanged words with them. They had got some way past the GPMG group when shots rang out. Up until this time all accounts of the unfortunate happenings that morning were in agreement, but precisely what happened in that instant at about 11.45 is still even today somewhat doubtful. Initial statements told of one or two shots coming from the direction of the RC Church followed by a rapid three round burst from the GPMG. It was this supposed 'crossfire' which caused the original misleading reports, but of the result there was no doubt: Majella O'Hare, a twelve-year-old girl lay in the middle of the road mortally wounded with gunshot wounds. She was immediately attended by soldiers and by a nurse, who was one of the four people who had been in the churchyard, and then rushed by helicopter to the Daisyhill Hospital, Newry where she arrived very quickly. But by 12.10 in the casualty department there, she was pronounced dead.

The task remained to discover exactly what occurred. The wounds which Majella had received were two small entry holes in her back with two larger (exit) wounds in her front abdomen. This indicated quite conclusively that the bullets which killed her came from behind, that is from the GPMG which was the only Army weapon to be fired. Several Marines and soldiers spoke under caution of one or two shots preceding the GPMG

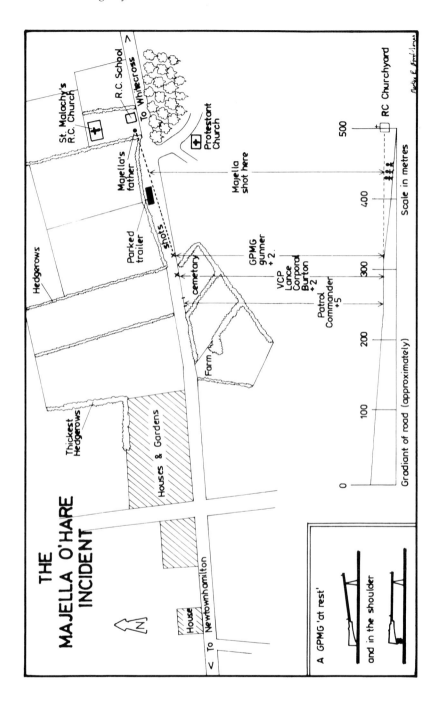

THE
MAJELLA O'HARE
INCIDENT

St. Malachy's R.C. Church
R.C. School
To Whitecross
Protestant Church
Majella's father
Parked trailer
shots
Majella shot here
Hedgerows
GPMG gunner +2
cemetary
VCP Lance Corporal Burton +2
Patrol Commander +5
Farm
Thickest Hedgerows
Houses & Gardens
House
To Newtownhamilton
RC Churchyard

Scale in metres
0    100    200    300    400    500
Gradient of road (approximately)

A GPMG 'at rest'
and in the shoulder

fire and Mr Reavey initially also thought that the first firing came from elsewhere but the determination of the direction from which shots come is notoriously difficult to judge, particularly when there are buildings and hills which can reflect the noise of firing with misleadingly convincing echoes.

The GPMG gunner's story was straightforward and he never wavered from it. He was quite adamant that he saw a gunman at a gap in the hedge which surrounded the RC Churchyard and on seeing this man he instantaneously cried out, raised his weapon to the shoulder, cocked it and fired. The more he reflected on the event over the next few weeks (and I personally spent a lot of time talking to him) the more he came to accept that the gunman did not fire at him first and that his action was so instantaneous that he could not have achieved a good sight picture, for had he done so he would surely have seen the young girls and boys. Without any question something moving caused him to cock the weapon in the first place and he was never shaken from his conviction that he saw a gunman in the gap in the churchyard hedge. Indeed subsequently a tracker dog, run from the point where the 'gunman' was seen, cast a very convincing trail to the east along a concealed route which led to a road and which could not have been observed by any of the soldiers.

As Majella lay mortally wounded in the road her father appeared from the churchyard where he had been cutting the grass in approximately the area where the GPMG gunner had seen his gunman. A further oddity was that two of the girls, Una and Caroline Murphy (aged sixteen and fourteen) reported seeing a soldier climbing down the bank in front of them, that is between them and the churchyard, at the moment that Majella was shot. If their recollection is accurate this could only have been the gunman for no soldier was nearer to them than the GPMG gun group but a more likely explanation is that by the time they had collected their thoughts at least two soldiers were amongst and beyond them and one was trying to stem Majella's bleeding. Whatever the reasoning it is quite clear that the tragic death of twelve-year-old Majella at the hands of 3 PARA was both accidental and very embarrassing to the battalion and to the Army.

Quite understandably 3 PARA was castigated by the press,

partly for killing Majella but more for producing conflicting versions of the event, and we were even accused of organising a cover up. From my point of view there was no intention to do other than tell the truth from the beginning, but as in so many events which take place in a mere flash of time initial reports are always incomplete and often quite misleading. Sometimes it is possible to with-hold a statement until after the dust has settled and you are reasonably certain of the true sequence of events, but in this instance because it was such a newsworthy event that was never on the cards, the pressure right from the beginning was for an immediate statement. On Sunday 22nd August the *Sunday Times* carried a stinging article which accurately described the incident, but totally ignored the Army's duty to defend its soldiers one or more of whom might eventually have to face a prosecution. The article's last words quoting Mr James O'Hare are probably the most perceptive: 'If it was an accident, then I could understand it, when soldiers carry guns, obviously accidents can happen. But I do not feel at the moment that I'm being told the truth.' The DPP subsequently considered the evidence and the GPMG gunner was tried on a charge of manslaughter and in April 1977 he was thankfully acquitted.

How the soldier managed to shoot a young innocent girl instead of the gunman is relatively easy to rationalise. He was on the brow of a hill and the churchyard was below him but slightly above the level of the road, so his line of sight to the gunman would have been above his sight line to the group of children. He would have been in the prone position with the gun at rest, that is with the butt of the weapon rested on the ground. In his excitement of seeing a gunman he had to carry out five very rapid actions which from his training were second nature to him, these were to raise the butt to the shoulder, cock the weapon, shout a warning, take aim and fire. This whole sequence can be completed in about three seconds but any lesser time will effect the accuracy of the sight picture. The soldier had only, in his keenness to protect his comrades, to squeeze his trigger a fraction of a second before he had obtained that clear sight picture and the bullets would have gone astray. This is what could so easily have occurred in this case. The difference between tragedy and success could not be more clearly illustrated when measured in fractions of a second.

\*

The last two days of the tour flashed past. Sunday, 15th August was quiet except for a huge fire in a furniture store in Bessbrook village which showered sparks over the whole area in the early hours, and on Monday an 80 lb IED was cleared on the Dublin Road. The newspapers on both days were full of the Majella O'Hare case and I felt embarrassed, even humiliated. On Monday we had intended to hold a drinks party for the RUC officers with whom we had worked for four months but I cancelled it, having decided that it would do the RUC no good at all if it ever became known that we had had a party together at a time when they were investigating the Ballymoyer shooting. Instead I made a brief visit to my Chief Superintendent's home to thank him and his wife for their hospitality and to deliver a bottle of whisky. I considered myself very privileged to have been associated with such a splendid couple who were the epitome of everything that is good in Northern Ireland.

The changeover day, Tuesday 17th August, was clear and sunny and everything ran like clockwork. The forward helicopter landing site proved very successful and I handed over to Julian Thompson at 11.15 and by 12.10 I had finally washed my hands of South Armagh. On my way to Belfast I called in at Portadown to see Brigadier David Woodford to brief him on the latest developments in the Majella O'Hare case. He told me that the GOC was considering changing our last press release but I persuaded him that this would only cause further confusion and later events bore out the logic of this argument.

My leave taken I drove to the Belfast docks from where we sailed at 19.45 on the landing ship *Sir Geraint*. It was a superbly calm crossing, the sort of evening when it would have been nice to celebrate the end of a successful tour, so it was doubly unfortunate that we had so very little to celebrate. I had arranged that soldiers who lived in the north should go straight on leave from Liverpool leaving the remainder who lived in the south (largely the married men) to travel to Aldershot in the convoy of our vehicles or by special train. Everyone was back there by 16.00 and the whole battalion had departed on leave by 17.00.

From Liverpool Corporal Mitchum drove me to Worksop to see the Boruckis. I had not warned them of the visit because I was unsure about the timing but fortunately they were both at home and pleased to see me. They were obviously very cut up about John's death and the father particularly was evidently very close to him. Now a coalminer he had arrived in England with the Polish Army and had fought with the Polish Parachutists in the Second World War. A splendid and diminutive character he epitomised the spirit of that force, his homeland, and the mining community in which he now lived. He was clearly very proud of his son's achievement in becoming a member of 3 PARA, and that made his loss all the more difficult to accept. I was able to reassure them that his death was not in any way his own fault nor the fault of any member of 3 PARA. I spent an hour with them and then set off for Aldershot where I arrived at 14.30.

Just short of Aldershot, my heart nearly stopped. Approaching some traffic lights at Bagshot I noticed a landrover upside down at the side of the road with a member of 3 PARA standing beside it. The vehicle had capsized largely because the driver had been travelling far too fast, but fortunately no one had been injured. I thought that perhaps our luck had changed; on our track record in South Armagh we could have expected a somewhat different result.

# Epilogue

The Majella O'Hare killing cast a cloud which was destined to hang over 3 PARA's reputation for some time to come. Certainly I took her death very personally (I had, after all, three daughters of my own) and my shame was heightened to some extent because it was considered unwise for me to do what my conscience dictated, which was to visit the O'Hares and apologise. Had I done so it would almost inevitably have prejudiced a soldier's fair trial, but I had no doubt that I would have felt happier, and so I think would the O'Hares.

Just as I had supported the rest of my men who had made well intentioned mistakes during the tour, so I now supported this one and did everything in my power to see that he was treated fairly, indeed I resisted the pressure from HQNI to imprison him pending trial and personally guaranteed that he would not abscond. But inside I was really sick that one incident, in the space of barely a second, had almost totally wiped out the good things that 3 PARA had achieved in South Armagh. Occurring as it did right at the very end of our tour, the incident falsely coloured the final verdict on our efforts, and served to remind people of our other failures: the SAS border crossing; the death of another innocent, Liam Prince, and of Constable Johnson; the unnecessary gunshot injuries to Privates Hastings, Evans and Lee; the murders of Privates Snowdon and Borucki and RUC Sergeant Hunter; the stupid loss of a pistol; and the injuries through terrorism to several civilians, RUC and UDR men. Against these our successes were all too easily forgotten. The tour which had promised so much at the outset was at the final reckoning just another in a long line. All the energy, dedication and determination had unfortunately done little to improve South Armagh and even Paddy, normally pretty supportive, was stingingly critical of the Majella O'Hare incident and our subsequent handling of it.

Highly self-critical myself and perhaps over-sensitive to criticism from others I have often reflected upon whether the outcome of the tour was an inevitable result of my approach. I had decided right back in January before we started training that we would take a positive and high profile line during our tour, but I could alternatively have decided that we would do as little as we could get away with, or that I would impose so many constraints as to stifle individual enterprise and initiative. Some took one or both options and their battalions consequently generated less publicity and had fewer 'accidents'. Possibly the deaths of Liam Prince, Constable Johnson, Majella O'Hare and even Snowdon and Borucki could be the direct results of my policy. It is certainly a feasible thesis but it ignores our collective conscience. Could or should a Parachute battalion go to South Armagh where its role was to support the RUC in its most difficult and dangerous area and take such a passive and unimaginative line? I thought not, and certainly my men had no doubts. Indeed I have not changed in my mind with the benefit of hindsight; if I had my time over again I would not alter anything – except our luck.

With very few exceptions every one of my officers and men went to South Armagh with a burning desire to accept the challenge and with the sincere intention of carrying out their unusual and demanding role sympathetically and intelligently. To this end they were content cheerfully to risk their lives and in the process two of their young comrades were brutally murdered. Occasionally frightened, happy, or excited but more often tired and bored the tour passed differently for each member according to his personal circumstances and role, but at the end they could each feel very satisfied that they had given of their best and enjoyed a comradeship forged in adversity and which is second to none. For almost all of them it was the best tour they had experienced in Ulster, and it was one which they would not easily forget.

Seen from my perspective I was just saddened that so much good and so much really hard work had been tarnished by a few unfortunate occurrences. Added together the thinking

*Lance-Corporal Cochrane and Private Holberry of B Company entertaining the children of Camlough village.*

time which resulted in the deaths of two innocent people in two separate incidents was not more than 10 seconds and probably much less, but it was those seconds which tended to eclipse the other 10.7 million seconds of the four months. I had always hoped that 3 PARA's tour would be noteworthy but I have to confess to some disappointment that the noteworthiness took the form it did.

Thus concluded an emergency roulement tour which was both typical and atypical and I hope that I have succeeded in conveying a flavour of what a tour means to the participants. The result was typical but the brilliant weather and some of the incidents were most unusual. Battalions going to Northern Ireland know full well that they cannot win or achieve a victory, for the situation there is not one for solution by military means. Nevertheless and despite this knowledge we all hanker for 'success', whatever that is, or acclaim and yet many return to the mainland disappointed, frustrated and occasionally chastened. Luckily this feeling does not last for very long and in no time at all each battalion is raring to have another go, such is the resilience of human endeavour. Somewhere in each of us who give it any thought at all is the hope that in an English speaking Christian island with a long democratic tradition and close ties to Britain, commonsense must eventually prevail. The fact is of course that most people there are sensible, hospitable and peaceable but in the six counties which today comprise Northern Ireland that majority seem to have surrendered through apathy, fear or intimidation to the murderous or vociferous hard core of evil men and women, Protestant and Catholic, who are determined that Ireland shall forever be in turmoil.

For myself and despite the frustrations and disappointments I was delighted with 3 PARA. They were still in my view the best battalion in the Army and it had been a great privilege to command them during such a challenging and worthwhile enterprise. Nothing before or since has rivalled for me those stimulating and sometimes exciting months of our tour in South Armagh.

As we left the Province we received the normal clutch of formal thank you letters and telegrams. Understandably, given the embarrassment of the last few days, none sounded genuinely effusive and from the RUC there was silence. I was not surprised, in their shoes I would have felt the same way. The taste which it all left was rather sour and the nicest compliment we received came from H. Jones, untarnished by the O'Hare death. Proceeding on leave two days before she was so tragically killed he had written to me before setting off as follows:

> I thought I should write now to thank you and 3 PARA for all you have done in the last four months. I was naturally slightly apprehensive before 3 PARA arrived, since I obviously hoped for great things from the battalion – but I need not have worried. The battalion's performance throughout the tour has made me proud to have once served in it; there is no doubt in my mind that you are the most successful battalion we have ever had in South Armagh.

From a man like H, who was later to become a household name when he was awarded a posthumous Victoria Cross, that was praise indeed, but I always wondered what he would have

*The face of South Armagh. A bewildered local inspecting the damage after a terrorist landmine explosion near Crossmaglen.*

written, indeed whether he would have written at all, if his departure on leave had been three days later. A week in Northern Ireland (as in politics) is a long time.

The Regular Army has always maintained a small garrison in Northern Ireland which over the last now almost two decades has been strengthened and further reinforced by successions of units on emergency roulement tours such as the one which I have described. These tours impose a serious interruption to the normal cycle of training for general war and some strain upon the family and social lives of those involved. But it is all very tolerable, and with few exceptions the dedicated officers and men revel in the challenge of an unpredictable four months. Republicans often complain that the resultant military presence is the overbearing and overt manifestation of the British holding down a reluctant Province by force of arms, but nothing could be further from the truth. We cannot have civil war in a part of the United Kingdom so the solution lies entirely in their hands, and those of the Loyalist para-militaries.

When terrorism stops and the Republicans revert to peaceful methods of pursuing their perfectly legitimate desires of a united Ireland and the Loyalists pursue their opposing aims in a similarly democratic fashion, then the threat of civil war will recede and emergency roulement tours can be terminated.

When this happens the British Army will breathe a sigh of relief but until that time I feel confident that its officers and men will continue to accept, benefit from and even enjoy their visits to the beautiful but troubled land which is Northern Ireland.

# Synopsis of Incidents

(Not including 23 hoax bombs, 70 reports of shots heard, 10 reports of explosions heard, 17 instances of minor aggro including stoning, 8 armed robberies, 233 arrests (planned, speculative and in hot pursuit)).

| Date | Time | Event | Chapter |
|------|------|-------|---------|
| Thu 15 Apr | 10.07 | 3 PARA assumed responsibility for military support to RUC in South Armagh | 3 |
| | 19.45 | A Wessex helicopter landing at CROSSMA-GLEN was hit by an RPG 7 and small arms fire. The Wessex limped back to BESS-BROOK later | 4 |
| | 23.25 | An SAS patrol earlier arrested Peter Joseph Cleary of BELLEEK. He was shot dead when he assaulted the patrol commander whilst waiting to be extracted by helicopter just south of FORKILL. | 4 |
| Fri 16 Apr | 03.25 | Cleary's body released to Daisyhill Hospital, NEWRY. | 4 |
| | 16.26 | Patrol found 23 feet of safety fuse near CAMLOUGH. | – |
| | 19.28 | 50 men in para military uniforms escorted Cleary's body from NEWRY to BELLEEK. | 4 |
| Sat 17 Apr | 20.15 | RUC patrol car shot at in NEWRY. | – |
| | 21.35 | Vehicle patrol in DERRYBEG Estate, NEWRY found two pistols lying in the road. | 4 |
| Sun 18 Apr | 01.42 | Small bomb containing 15 lbs of home made explosive defused at the ROSTREVOR Yacht Club. | – |
| | am & pm | Easter Sunday Marches in six different locations passed peacefully. | 4 |

| Date | Time | Event | Chapter |
|------|------|-------|---------|
| Mon 19 Apr | 14.36 | Peter Cleary's funeral in BELLEEK. All those attending questioned on their way from the service. | 4 |
| Tue 20 Apr | 14.07 | Bomb containing 15 lbs of gelignite defused on the railway line North of NEWRY. | 4 |
| | 17.20 | Eight shots fired at HMS ALERT on station in CARLINGFORD LOUGH from the Republic. | – |
| | 18.40 | An attempt to stop a Northbound express just North of the border failed. The terrorist fired about 20 rounds. | 4 |
| Wed 21 Apr | 19.59 | One shot fired at a patrol outside the GLENANNE base. The gunmen escaped by car. | 4 |
| Thu 22 Apr | 13.07 | One shot fired at a patrol in the DERRYBEG Estate, NEWRY. | – |
| | 14.06 | One shot fired at a patrol near DRUMINTEE. | – |
| | 21.15 | Following a sighting of two armed men in a car near MOUNTAINHOUSE, East of BELLEEK three rounds were fired at the patrol who returned fire. It was thought that one terrorist had been wounded. | 4 |
| Sat 24 Apr | 14.35 | One round fired at a patrol South of WHITECROSS at 800 metres range. The gunman escaped towards BELLEEK. | – |
| | 22.40 | An explosion in the Ulster Bar, WARREN-POINT seriously injured one person and a further 20 were taken to hospital. It was estimated that 30 lbs of explosive were used. | |
| | 22.47 | Two large fires were started in NEWRY. Several shops were destroyed. | 5 |
| Sun 25 Apr | 17.41 | Five rounds were fired at a patrol near MEIGH. | 5 |
| | 19.20 | Over 60 rounds were fired at a patrol near MILLTOWN, SE of CROSSMAGLEN. The patrol returned the fire (250 rounds) and claimed one terrorist hit. This was confirmed on 3 May when the Garda arrested Colm Murphy in hospital in Dundalk. One bullet struck a soldier's rifle, knocking it from his hands. | 5 |
| Tue 27 Apr | 06.10 | Morris 1100 containing 120 lbs of home made explosive and 10 lbs of Frangex defused on the Dublin Road just South of NEWRY. | 5 |
| | 10.50 | Shots were fired at a soldier supervising quarry blasting South of NEWRY. Eleven rounds of fire were returned. | 5 |

| Date | Time | Event | Chapter |
|------|------|-------|---------|
| Wed 28 Apr | 16.30 | Two shots were fired at a CROSSMAGLEN base sangar. In the follow up Private Hastings shot himself in the foot. | 5 |
| | 23.45 | A recently vacated OP on the border near CLONTYGORA (H3) was attacked. No soldiers were within 500 metres. On examining the site the following day 217 assorted empty cases were found together with the remains of 3 pipe bombs. At least 4 terrorists must have been involved in the assault. | 5 |
| Thu 29 Apr | 20.40 | One shot fired at the NEWRY base sangar. | – |
| Fri 30 Apr | 12.10 | One shot fired at a permanent VCP in NEWRY town centre. | – |
| | 16.41 | A patrol near H34 (NW OF CROSSMAGLEN) had about 8 rounds fired at it from the Republic. The patrol fired back (only 2 rounds) but there was no follow up due to the border. | – |
| Sat 1 May | 12.00 | A patrol had about 12 rounds fired at it by two gunmen near the Post Office in CULLYHANNA. The gunmen escaped by car towards the border. | 7 |
| | 16.37 | Four gunmen were seen by a patrol at MONOG, just South of CROSSMAGLEN. The patrol fired two rounds and the gunmen escaped. 18 rounds of ammunition were found in the follow up. | 7 |
| Tue 4 May | 01.10 | An 80 lb device was detonated behind a garden wall in NEWRY. Six civilians were taken to hospital with minor injuries. | 7 |
| | 14.35 | One shot fired at a patrol in NEWRY. | 7 |
| Wed 5 May | 08.40 | Large VCP operation implemented in an attempt to re-capture escapers from the Maze Prison. | 7 |
| | 10.57 | One shot fired at a patrol in the BALLIN-TEMPLE area (3 miles S of CAMLOUGH). | – |
| | 22.50 | Two SAS soldiers were arrested in the Republic South of H2 after making a map reading error. | 7 |
| Thu 6 May | 02.00 | A further six SAS soldiers were arrested in the Republic. | 7 |
| Fri 7 May | 11.30 | RUC and Army explosives escort crossed border accidentally in area H5 (the main Dublin Road). | 7 |
| | 22.31 | A bomb consisting of about 30 lbs of home made explosive exploded at Tully's Bar in BELLEEK. Miraculously no one was injured. | 7 |

| Date | Time | Event | Chapter |
|------|------|-------|---------|
| Sun 9 May | 00.09 | A car proxy bomb consisting of about 100 lbs of home made explosive was defused at the NEWRY RUC station. | 7 |
| | 05.20 | In a covert operation 4 milkchurns containing a total of 900 lbs of home made explosive were defused just SW of CAMLOUGH. | 7 |
| Tue 11 May | 20.05 | Two armed men seen driving away from a farmhouse SW of BELLEEK turned out subsequently to be RUC men in plain clothes. | – |
| Sat 15 May | 09.37 | A routine patrol at FLURRYBRIDGE (H7) found 7 beer kegs each containing 100 lbs of home made explosive at Mullens Garage, which straddles the border. | 8 |
| | 23.43 | An RUC civilianised patrol car was ambushed on the main road just NW of WARRENPOINT. Sgt Hunter was killed and two reserve constables were seriously injured. Ten empty Armalite cases were found the following day. | 8 |
| Sun 16 May | 20.30 | Two gunmen fired three rounds at the mobile Dublin Road VCP. Fire was returned (59 rounds) but no hits were claimed. | 8 |
| | 21.35 | The same VCP was again attacked. Five rounds were fired by the terrorists and 27 rounds were returned. | 8 |
| Tue 18 May | 16.28 | In an explosion near H28 a 5 foot crater was blown on the hillside and a horse was slightly injured. | – |
| Sat 22 May | 00.25 | A patrol near H13A found two beer kegs of home made explosive in a derelict building. These were defused the following day and found to contain over 200 lbs of explosive. With them was a red flag, presumably for stopping trains on the nearby railway. | 8 |
| Tue 25 May | 13.25 | Car bomb of an estimated 75 lbs exploded in central NEWRY after a 30 minute warning. Seven shops were badly damaged. | – |
| | 17.50 | Puma helicopter overflew border at 11.25. | 8 |
| | 18.35 | Four man patrol arrested by Garda after crossing border accidentally near H25. | 8 |
| Fri 28 May | 23.30 | Warning telephoned of a bomb in the CAMLOUGH Sludge Clearance Factory. It was found in the ladies lavatory and defused on 30 May and found to contain 24 lbs Frangex and a timing device. | – |

| Date | Time | Event | Chapter |
|------|------|-------|---------|
| Sun 30 May | 02.58 | An RUC vehicle patrol travelling on the main road two miles NW of WARRENPOINT had about 20 rounds fired at it from the Republic. | – |
| Tue 8 June | 09.20 | Corporal John Heasley of 3 UDR was shot and seriously injured (9 gunshot wounds) at his workplace in NEWRY. Two of his workmates were also injured but all eventually recovered. | 10 |
| Wed 9 June | 16.05 | An Irish Army football team accidentally crossed the border near CULLAVILLE. | 10 |
| | 21.00 | Two Garda accidentally crossed the border near H9. | 10 |
| Sat 12 June | 23.15 | A large landmine consisting of 200 lbs of home made explosive was detonated about 15 metres to the rear of the last man of a foot patrol near DRUMINTEE. In the subsequent events Liam Prince of WARRENPOINT was mistakenly shot dead. | 10 |
| Thu 17 June | 11.30 | An Irish Army Cessna aircraft accidentally crossed the border. | – |
| Tue 22 June | 17.23 | In an explosion triggered by radio control Private William Snowdon was fatally wounded and two others were injured. The incident occurred near H40 and about 40 lbs of commercial explosive was used. | 10 |
| Wed 23 June | 09.53 | Two armed men were seen near GLASDRUMMAN (one mile N of H24) by a foot patrol who opened fire at long range. The terrorists escaped. | 10 |
| Thu 24 June | 09.42 | Two armed people (one male, one female) placed a small device which was later defused in the office of the NEWRY Reporter. | – |
| | 16.35 | A van containing three youths from CROSSMAGLEN armed with replica pistols was stopped and the occupants arrested. | 10 |
| Fri 25 June | 21.52 | Three gunmen were captured and a further gunman wounded in an incident near the MOUNTAINHOUSE INN. | 10 |
| Sat 26 June | 22.00 | About 20 rounds were fired from the Republic at a Rigid Raider from HMS ALERT in CARLINGFORD LOUGH. | 10 |
| Tue 6 Jul | 08.20 | An explosion caused a large crater in the Concession Road at CULLAVILLE. It was triggered by Sergeant Lucey who had connected a radio battery to two wires. | 11 |

| Date | Time | Event | Chapter |
|------|------|-------|---------|
| | 14.00 | Privates Lee and Hassell were involved in an incident at the Horseshoe Bar, LISBURN. Lee was shot in the shoulder and a pistol was stolen. | 11 |
| Wed 7 Jul | 02.00 | One shot was fired at a patrol outside the CROSSMAGLEN base. Fire was returned but no hits were claimed. | – |
| | 10.30 | Two armed men entered Fishers Timber Yard in NEWRY. Their intended target, Major James Henning of 3 UDR escaped by jumping through a window. Another employee was seriously wounded by gunfire. | 11 |
| Thu 8 Jul | 01.30 | Four masked and armed men took over the public house in CREGGAN and placed explosives in the building. It was not until Wed 21 Jul that we disarmed several devices by burning out the building. | 11 |
| Mon 12 Jul | 16.19 | Two youths placed a 3 lb bomb in a butchers shop in NEWRY. A drunk threw it into the street where it was later disarmed. | – |
| Tue 13 Jul | 09.31 | Two shots were fired at a compromised patrol on the border between H19 and H21. In the follow up two milkchurns with about 120 lbs of explosive and a timing device were disarmed in a bomb making 'factory'. | 11 |
| | 18.40 | Between 100 and 200 rounds were fired at HMS VIGILANT from the Republic as she left the dockside at WARRENPOINT. Fire was returned but the only casualty was an innocent civilian who was hit by splinters caused by the terrorist's fire. | 11 |
| Sat 17 Jul | 15.20 | A bug was discovered in Eileesh Morley's house in NEWRY. | 11 |
| Sun 18 Jul | 00.23 | 4-8 Mortar bombs were fired at the NEWRY base. None hit but there was some slight damage to civilian property. | 11 |
| Mon 19 July | 15.30 | 118 rounds (some of which were armour piercing) were found in a hollow tree on the border near H25. | 11 |
| | 15.55 | A rifle with 150 rounds was found in ivy on top of a wall in NEWRY. | 11 |
| Tue 20 Jul | 06.55 | Private Evans shot himself in the stomach whilst fiddling with a pistol at BESSBROOK. | 12 |
| | 21.50 | Eight shots were fired from the Republic at the permanent OP overlooking FLURRYBRIDGE (H7). Fire was returned (135 rounds) and the Garda later arrested five men. | 12 |

| Date | Time | Event | Chapter |
|------|------|-------|---------|
| Thu 22 Jul | 12.06 | About 8 rounds were fired at an armoured personnel carrier in the DERRYBEG Estate, NEWRY. | – |
| Fri 23 Jul | 15.35 | A planned search near H19 found a suspected IED. When it was disarmed the following day it was found to consist of a clip of ammunition connected to a 30 lbs booby trap. | 12 |
| | 17.24 | A 'proxy bomb' in a car was delivered to FORKILL base. This led to another device hidden in a trailer piled with straw bales some 100 metres away. That device was defused by burning and consisted of 30 lbs of home made explosive. | 12 |
| | 18.20 | Two wires found some time previously near GLASDRUMMAN were pulled on a long rope which caused two craters in the road. | – |
| Sat 24 Jul | 09.50 | About 13 shots were fired at the NEWRY base sentry who returned fire. The terrorists were thought to have escaped by car to nearby estate. | 12 |
| | 14.20 | One shot at a patrol in the Market area of NEWRY hit a Mrs Jennings in the arm. | 12 |
| | 18.35 | The Medical Officer's armoured personnel carrier was hit by small arms fire near the DERRYBEG Estate, NEWRY. | 12 |
| | 21.37 | Three shots were fired at long range at a patrol near KINGSMILLS in the North of our area. | 12 |
| Sun 25 Jul | 01.10 | An incendiary device gutted a shop in NEWRY. | 12 |
| | 02.22 | A further shop was gutted in NEWRY. | 12 |
| Mon 26 Jul | 06.00 | During a planned search in NEWRY some terrorist equipment (including detonators) was found in a house. Three men were arrested. | – |
| Thu 29 Jul | 01.33 | RUC Reserve Constable Johnson was shot dead by the BESSBROOK sentry. | 12 |
| | 01.49 | An anonymous telephone call warned of two car bombs in NEWRY. At 02.19 a white Ford Transit Van exploded. There were no casualties but some structural damage to shops. It was estimated that the device consisted of about 200 lbs of home made explosive. | 12 |
| Fri 30 Jul | 22.55 | Two shots were fired at the BESSBROOK VCP sentry by a car passenger. | 12 |

| Date | Time | Event | Chapter |
|------|------|-------|---------|
| Sat 31 Jul | 01.50 | Eugene McCullough was knee capped in both legs in NEWRY. | 12 |
| | 06.12 | A booby trapped Army torch left by the CROSSMAGLEN base exploded when a patrol commander tried to 'pull' it. Four very minor casualties were taken to hospital. | 12 |
| Tue 3 Aug | 09.30 | Captain W E Tombs, 3 UDR was ambushed in NEWRY and wounded on his way to work. | 12 |
| Thu 5 Aug | 21.36 | Three shots were fired at the O'MEATH VCP from across the NEWRY River. | 12 |
| Fri 6 Aug | 06.00 | A hide in a wall near H25 was found and ambushed. | – |
| | 16.07 | A 100 lbs car bomb exploded outside the WARRENPOINT RUC Station. Damage was slight. | 12 |
| | 22.05 | 30-40 Armalite rounds were fired at the NEWRY base. Although fire was returned (16 rounds) no hits were claimed. | 12 |
| Sun 8 Aug | 16.15 | A radio controlled bomb in a bicycle exploded in CROSSMAGLEN killing Private John Borucki instantly. | 12 |
| | 21.00 | Two armoured personnel carriers belonging to 2 RRF crossed the border at H6 and were turned back by the Garda. | 12 |
| Mon 9 Aug | AM | Anniversary of Internment passed very quietly. | 13 |
| Tue 10 Aug | 21.20 | Three shots were fired at a patrol near FLURRYBRIDGE (H7) from the Republic. 66 rounds were fired back but no hits were claimed. | 13 |
| Wed 11 Aug | 08.20 | Two shotguns and 10 rounds of high velocity ammunition were found East of NEWRY. | – |
| Sat 14 Aug | 11.45 | A patrol near WHITECROSS accidentally shot dead Majella O'Hare. | 13 |
| | 15.45 | A 100 lbs device near H19 was neutralised. | – |
| Mon 16 Aug | 13.50 | An 80 lbs bomb on the Dublin Road, South of NEWRY was defused. | 13 |
| | 17.07 | East of NEWRY a pistol was found. | – |
| Tue 17 Aug | 11.25 | 3 PARA ceased responsibility for military support to the RUC in SOUTH ARMAGH. | 13 |

# Ammunition

Total ammunition expended during the tour was:

7.62 mm (rifle and GPMG ammunition)                    – 1137
9mm (sub machine gun ammunition)                       –   15
Baton rounds (plastic bullets)                         –   22
84 mm TPTP (anti-tank rounds for disrupting IEDs)      –    8
83 Grenades (coloured smoke for attracting helicopters) – 122

# Abbreviations and Initials Used

| | | |
|---|---|---|
| AAC | – | Army Air Corps |
| ACC | – | Assistant Chief Constable |
| ARF | – | Airborne Reaction Force (Scout helicopter + 6) |
| ATO | – | Ammunition Technical Officer (bomb disposal) |
| BBC | – | British Broadcasting Corporation |
| BAOR | – | British Army of the Rhine |
| CBE | – | Commander of the Order of the British Empire |
| CCTV | – | Close Circuit Television |
| CID | – | Criminal Investigation Department |
| CIVAD | – | Civil Affairs Adviser |
| CLF | – | Commander Land Forces (the Army General controlling all Army activity) |
| CO | – | Commanding Officer |
| COP | – | Close/Covert Observation Post/Platoon |
| DAC | – | District Action Committee |
| DHSS | – | Department of Health and Social Security |
| DMO | – | Director of Military Operations (an MOD appointment) |
| DPP | – | Director of Public Prosecutions |
| EEC | – | European Economic Community |
| Garda | – | Southern Irish Police Force |
| Gazelle | – | A small helicopter (4 passengers) |
| GOC | – | General Officer Commanding (the Senior Serviceman in Northern Ireland) |
| GPMG | – | General Purpose Machine Gun |
| GR | – | Grid Reference |

| | | |
|---|---|---|
| 1 Green Howards | – | 1st Battalion The Green Howards |
| H i to H43 | – | Numbering system for South Armagh border crossings |
| HLS | – | Helicopter Landing Site |
| HQ | – | Headquarter(s) |
| HQNI | – | Headquarters Northern Ireland (the main Army HQ) |
| HSB | – | Head of Special Branch (RUC) |
| ID Cards | – | Identity Cards |
| IED | – | Improvised Explosive Devices (a home-made bomb) |
| INLA | – | Irish National Liberation Army (Catholic) |
| IO | – | Intelligence Officer |
| IP | – | Information Policy |
| IRSP | – | Irish Republican Social Party (Catholic) |
| LMG | – | Light Machine Gun |
| LSC | – | Local Security Committee |
| LS | – | Landing Site (helicopter) |
| MG | – | Machine Gun |
| MIO | – | Military Intelligence Officer |
| MI5 | – | Military Intelligence 5 (the Security Service) |
| MOD | – | Ministry of Defence |
| MP | – | Member of Parliament |
| NATO | – | North Atlantic Treaty Organisation |
| NCO | – | Non-Commissioned Officer |
| NITAT | – | Northern Ireland Training and Advisory Team |
| OC | – | Officer Commanding |
| O Group | – | Orders Group |
| OIRA | – | Official Irish Republican Army (Catholic) |
| OP | – | Observation Point/Post |
| PARAs | – | Members of the Parachute Regiment |
| 2 PARA | – | 2nd Battalion The Parachute Regiment |
| 3 PARA | – | 3rd Battalion The Parachute Regiment |
| PIRA | – | Provisional Irish Republican Army |
| Puma | – | A Medium Sized Helicopter (16 passengers) |
| 1 QLR | – | 1st Battalion The Queen's Lancashire Regiment |
| QRF | – | Quick Reaction Force (a reserve available at each Base) |

| | | |
|---|---|---|
| R and R | – | Rest and Recuperation |
| RAF | – | Royal Air Force |
| RE | – | Royal Engineers |
| 1 RHF | – | 1st Battalion The Royal Highland Fusiliers |
| RIC | – | Reconnaissance Intelligence Centre (RAF photographic interpretation) |
| RM | – | Royal Marines |
| RMP | – | Royal Military Police |
| RN | – | Royal Navy |
| RPG 7 | – | Soviet Shoulder Launched anti-Tank Weapon |
| 2 RRF | – | 2nd Battalion The Royal Regiment of Fusiliers |
| 1 RS | – | 1st Battalion The Royals Scots |
| RSM | – | Regimental Sergeant Major |
| 4 RTR | – | 4th Royal Tank Regiment |
| RUC | – | Royal Ulster Constabulary |
| RUC H Div | – | The RUC's Police Division in South Armagh |
| SAM | – | Surface to Air Missile |
| SAS | – | Special Air Service |
| 22 SAS | – | 22nd Special Air Service Regiment |
| SB | – | Special Branch |
| Scout | – | Small helicopter (5 passengers) |
| SDLP | – | Social Democratic and Labour Party (Catholic) |
| SIB | – | Special Investigation Branch (RMP) |
| Sioux | – | Small helicopter (2 passengers) |
| SOCO | – | Scene of Crimes Officer (RUC) |
| SNCO | – | Senior Non-Commissioned Officer |
| SPG | – | Special Patrol Group (RUC) |
| TA | – | Territorial Army |
| TAOR | – | Tactical Area of Responsibility |
| TV | – | Television |
| UDR | – | Ulster Defence Regiment |
| 2 UDR | – | 2nd Battalion The Ulster Defence Regiment |
| 3 UDR | – | 3rd Battalion The Ulster Defence Regiment |
| UVF | – | Ulster Volunteer Force |
| VCP | – | Vehicle Check Point |
| Wessex | – | A Medium Sized Helicopter (14 passengers) |
| WRAC | – | Women Royal Army Corps |

# Index

Entries in *italics* indicate illustrations or maps.